CONFESSIONS OF A STRIPPING ACTRESS

A Memoir of Adult Entertainment, Showbiz and Men

by

Roxanna Bina

This book is dedicated to my husband and sweet children... It is this wild journey that has led me, ultimately, to you... my guardian angels.

Copyright © 2020 by Roxanna Bina
All rights reserved. No part of this publication may be reproduced, distributed, or transmitted in any form or by any means, including photocopying, recording, or other electronic or mechanical methods, without the prior written permission of the publisher, except in the case of brief quotations embodied in critical reviews and certain other noncommercial uses permitted by copyright law. For permission requests or ordering, contact:

Roxanna Bina
www.roxannabina.com

Also available as an E-book and Audiobook.

Printed in the United States of America
ISBN # 978-0-578-63245 - Library of Congress
ISBN E-book #978-1-7923-2966-1

Photographs courtesy of the author, York Entertainment, Demarko, Lisa Gourley, and Danny Fogarty. Kindly, send an email if I have forgotten to give a photo credit, so it shall be added promptly in future editions.

Cover photo/art/layout by Roxanna Bina

This book is memoir. It reflects the author's present recollections of experiences over time. Some names and characteristics have been changed, some events have been compressed, and some dialogue has been recreated. Some photos have been blurred out to maintain privacy.

CONTENTS

Author's Note	1
Introduction	3
PART ONE	7
1 Money, Cars, Clothes and Hoes	9
2 Showtime	13
3 Bitches	15
4 Burlesque	17
5 Clients	21
6 Japanese businessmen	23
7 Nerdy Engagement	25
8 Jack the Eye Doctor	27
9 Pour Some Sugar On Me	31
10 Make It Purple Rain	39
11 Whitey The Lawyer	43
12 Stalking State Trooper	47
13 Viviana and the Case of the Itching Powder	53
14 Heroine or Heroin?	55
15 Ride and Almost Die	57
16 Mother Angela	59
17 Charlotte the Harlot	61
18 Hot Drunk Twins	65

19 Patriots MILF   69
20 Sativa Goes On A Trip   71
21 ATM Stake-out   73
22 Bouncers   75
23 Saudi Exports   77
24 99 Problems… and the Liquor License was one of them   81
25 The Foxy Lady   83
26 Playboy   87

PART TWO   91
This Is Acting?   93
1 Suburban Barbie   95
2 MTV   97
3 Harlequin Studios   101
4 Nice Box   103
5 Winona's Butt Double   105
6 The Rockettes   107
7 Bratz Doll   109
8 Hocus Pocus   111
9 Bollywood, Here I Come!   113
10 CreditCards, Please   115
11 Chuck E. Sleaze   117
12 Make-Shift Boudoir   119
13 Sister Bear   121
14 Patricia Field   123
15 Brooklyn Bound   125
16 Troma-tic Stories   129

17 The Stoney Awards	131
18 Festivals with Troma	133
19 Troma's Edge TV	135
20 La Nouvelle Justine	139
21 Fetish Modeling	141
22 Troy Boy	143
23 Wall Street Guy	151
24 Chef Boy	155
25 Lofty Goals	157
26 Fox Force Five	161
27 Club Kids	165
28 Punk Not Dead, It Just Got Maced	169
29 Barnes Avenue Boys Club	175
30 Suspicions Grow	181
31 End of an Era	185
PHOTOGRAPHS	189
About The Author	197

AUTHOR'S NOTE

First off, I'd like to thank you for taking the time to read about a stranger's life. In this day and age, you're lucky if someone tunes in to hear what your name is, let alone read a goddamn novel about the person's life. It took me a long time to reveal to anyone my exotic dancing past, mainly because of the stigma attached to it. But, I'm here to make that stigma fade for the new generation. Using your body and looks as a tool to get ahead should not be frowned upon, but rather celebrated. Now, I'm not saying not to use your mind, but if you can use both mind and body creatively... well, the possibilities are endless for a fruitful future! People do it everyday, so why not you?

In some ways, stripping is like acting, there's just no long-winded Oscars speeches involved and the money can be better at times. It was difficult organizing this book, mainly because my acting experiences and stripping experiences happened separately, yet at parallel time frame, sort of like a double life. So, I have organized the book as two parts: Stripping and Acting -and not in any particular order or timeline.

Hopefully, you can come away from this book with wisdom (or a few brain cells less, depending on how you look at it) from a rebel teenager, insight into the life a stripper and struggling actress and above all, lots of laughs. Enjoy and if you happen to run into my parents- tell them not to read this.

INTRODUCTION

Being an actress requires many skills…. Scratch that. Actually, it requires virtually no skills. Being pretty- check. The drive for fame and fortune- check- actually, enough money to pay for my lifestyle is good enough, thankyouverymuch. Remembering your lines- check- wait actually… there are teleprompters and good editing to fix that! Get into the character- check. actually, you just have to be borderline schizo with a very inventive backstory. What I'm really trying to say is… you may have what it takes to be a great actress, but it may not necessarily make you an OSCAHH winner or more importantly, a STAR.

Let me introduce myself- I'm Roxanna Bina and I am a failed actress that turned to stripping to be able to become an actress. Stripping was the fuel and acting was the drive behind it. As time went on, stripping became more of main gig, although I never did really stop auditioning. I have been to more auditions during the course of my life than a cat has taken naps during the course of its entire life. I have also had several dozen callbacks and even less than that of jobs booked. But what exactly made me realize I'm a failed actress? When I woke up one day and realized I stopped getting auditions for roles I used to NOT get- Ha ha ha. No longer was I getting calls for the quirky starlet or the hot bimbo in the background (what can I say, at least I had range!). Nope. I was getting barely any auditions for the role of 'mom' and 'mature businesswoman', which I don't mind getting lumped into that category at all... but it made me realize, maybe this acting thing will never take off, after all. The underlying question is... would becoming a successful actress erase all my problems, insecurities and fears all of a sudden? Probably not, but it was my dream, until I started a family.

    The thing about having a family is that your priorities change. Everything is a group decision.... Every decision you make, affects the family in some way. For instance, if I take that audition in LA, I'll have to pull the kids out school that day, drive a long-ass two hours, get to said audition, wrangle the kids with snacks, toys and a marathon of annoying Caillou videos to sit still at the studio, audition without having the producers thinking you're super unprofessional for bringing the whole, damn family, smile and hope for the best, then re-pack the kids in the car and drive back home another two hours hoping not to hit traffic... so should I have taken that audition? YES, and YES! Why? Because if I hadn't, I will think about what if that was my big break while I'm laid up in a nursing home 40 years from now... That's why!

    Any who, as I get older, I'm a bit choosier, but still active in sending out resumes. Oh yes, the submissions of today are quite different from when I was in my teens and twenties during the late 1990s and early 2000s... Back then, we had to have a sleazy, professional photographer take our headshots, wait a week to have them developed, choose the best photo out of the bunch, wait another week, have a bunch printed as 8x10s, then type up a resume for the back on regular 8x10 paper, staple the resume to the back of the 8x10 headshot photo and then trim down the excess paper. PAIN IN THE ASS! But wait... there's more! Then, you had to send these headshots out by mail (and I had the fancy envelope with the window on one side for the photo to be visible even if it was sitting on a filthy, mess of a pile on a desk at an agency). But where oh where would you get the addresses of the agencies?? Google was not around, yet... much less a vast, internet like today. You had to buy the addresses from published books as any magazine bodega in NYC. Also, there was a weekly newspaper called Backstage (East and West) that would have all sorts of listings if you were not yet with an agent. $100 worth of stamps and envelopes and photos later, you would wait and wait for an actual phone call.

    Now, having a Rhode Island number would surely deter any casting agency to figure you're not worth chasing down, so buying a NYC number was just the ticket... you would buy an NYC number with voicemail and then, you would check said voicemail from your RI phone as many times as you'd like to see if you got any messages. See, if the casting people saw an NYC number, they were more apt to think it's a serious actress that made that ballsy move to NYC... wow, that chick has balls– let's hire her!

    The whole thing was like a preparing a 5-course meal... but I was rarely getting a meal at the end. Times have changed a lot... there's hardly any legwork anymore.... Today, you just send out submissions on various online sites like L.A. CASTING... with a click, you're done, and you wait. It's like microwaving a TV dinner... so goddamn easy. And even better, you just direct casting people to your Instagram or YouTube and you can even send a quick audition video through your iPhone instantly or have a FaceTime chat. AMAZING! Anyone can do it now... back then, I would take a Greyhound bus to NYC from my hometown of Providence, Rhode Island (a three hour trip each way) after working the night before at the club and lug all my portfolios (like an actual photo album of all my modeling photos) that weighed probably as much the chubbiest, newborn twins from agency to agency in NYC. Winter- it was bone-chilling... summer- it was sweltering, especially the subways... it was WORK going from agency to agency, audition to audition, go-see to go-see all across NYC, not to mention going to college and dancing in strip clubs for cash.

In some ways, I wish I had it easy with just sending links out everywhere from the comfort of my living room, but then I think about it and have to say I lived my best life as a stripper/model/actress during the new golden age of NYC- pre-9/11... this was the late 1990s and early 2000s... when NYC was still the hub of downtown club kids, a grimy, crime-infested Brooklyn, a prosperous, coke-fueled Wall Street, hip-hop music blasting in the streets, the smell of roasted peanuts and drunk people urine wafting through the alleyways and underbelly of the city...and of course, the Analog age...no smartphones, no insta-anything and just pure energy to make it... here are some anecdotes from a small town, stripped down girl lost in the big city with boundless dreams to make it, no matter what....

PART ONE

CHAPTER 1
MONEY, CARS, CLOTHES & HOES

I was always fascinated with glamour, high heels and money. So, turning to stripping – wait, I hate that word- let's call it exotic dancing. So, turning to exotic dancing was a logical step for me. I just had graduated high school and remember asking my mom what she would think if I became a dancer. She shot that idea down instantly. She said she didn't want me to have a bad reputation. It was at that moment I knew I must never tell her or my family. See, I never listen to anyone, which could be good or bad depending on how you see it. My parents and my older brother emigrated from Iran during the early 1970s, well before the Iranian Revolution. Both are highly educated, intellectual types, so you can imagine the horror of them ever finding out their only daughter is an exotic dancer. Sometimes you gotta go the street smart way to beat the system, you know?

How did I get introduced to exotic dancing? It is a terrifying thought for a teenager. I had barely kissed a boy. I was having lunch with a couple of older guy friends in college and they always talked about strip clubs that they would go to. I asked them, would I be able to dance? Like am I hot enough? Do you have to have side-show size boobs to dance? Would the guys heckle me? And most importantly, how much money could I make in a night? You know, RANDOM questions like that. They told me I would be a perfect candidate and to go to an amateur night at one of the local clubs.

So, after a couple of days of thinking about how to go about dancing without having my family find out, I decided to do it. I had to pay for my headshots and bus money somehow. It was expensive being me! I clearly remember the day I went to a club in Providence. At the time, I had no idea which clubs were skanky, and which were classy. I had picked up the local Phoenix paper and look at the skeezy ads in the back part of the paper and saw all the clubs advertising their "Amateur Night", usually it would fall on their slowest nights, like on a Monday or Tuesday.

I chose a club named Cherry's. I thought the name was cute. Apparently, and I found this out later, that was a skanky club. I had brought a couple of my guy friends with me in case shit went down. It was the daytime and the high school across the street had just gotten out. Nice. We walk in and ask to talk to the manager, which was some dude with a Rastafarian look (I later run into him years later at Mario's. He was the boyfriend of this dancer with a padlock on her who- ha- no joke!). Let's call him Hey Mon.

So, Hey Mon asks me to come backstage to get some info from me. Have I danced before? What is my schedule like? Etc., etc. Meanwhile, my two guy friends are waiting in the club for me watching this chick take a shower on stage while 3- 4 elderly men were watching in the audience nursing their drinks- it was kind of hilarious. My friends were laughing hysterically, barely containing themselves. Hey Mon, asked me if I could return later that night, but I said no and that I would call him later. I really said no because it was going too fast for me and I had a feeling this was one of those skanky clubs. I decided to try out the other clubs and feel it out first. After I left, I reckon Hey Mon knew I wouldn't be coming back considering I didn't have saggy boobs and a c-section scar. I remember coming out of the club with my friends thinking, what the hell am I doing? Then, I remembered how much a dancer would make. It was typically $200 on a real shitty night and $1000 on a good night. Sounded good to me....better then waitressing for coins.

I knew that if I stayed a waitress at the neighborhood diner, Newport Creamery, I would never be able to buy a car, a house, or save for a Chanel suit. I calculated I needed to waitress 5 days a week/8 hour a day/ for 20 years before I could buy a car. Eff that!

And so, the amateur nights were calling me. But there was one thing I needed to do before I started at my new exciting job to make sure I was qualified. And that was to experience sex. If I were to sell the *illusion* of sex then I was going to have to do my research ... and so, I asked one of my best guy friends to de-flower me in the name of research during one school day at Rhode Island College. It was a crisp, late fall day and I remember I wanted to do it between classes at his dorm room while his roommate was away at class. It was quick, efficient and underwhelming. Also, I wore a pink wig for some strange reason that day. I remember thinking all the fuss in society for sex is about *THAT*?! Almost immediately after, I put back on my clothes and made it in time for Chemistry class. My friend was happy to help, but things got weird with him fast. In any case, I was ready to tackle the job like a pro, or so I thought.

One night I was sitting in my bedroom calling a few of the clubs. I figured if I danced in Providence, I may run into people I know which would be a travesty, especially since my family shouldn't know. My dad had left for California and my parents were going through a divorce. So, my dad was out of the picture, which was a relief in some ways. The rules in the house were more lenient without my dad and it was an overall less stressful atmosphere at home with my mom and dad apart. If you ever happen to see the film "The War of the Roses" with Danny DeVito, Michael Douglas and Kathleen Turner, that is exactly how my parents' divorce transpired… vindictive and full of drama.

Anyway, I saw an ad for a brand-new club opening in nearby Johnston called 'Mario's Showplace'. When I called to see if they were hiring dancers, a really nice lady was on the other end, as opposed to some mob-sounding guy at the other clubs. I actually felt safe. So, I went in and met with Marion and Frank, who would both later play a significant part during my exotic dancing career. Frank was a stout man with a stern mafia look in his 50s, but with a heart of gold. Marion was a former dancer in her 30s and was wife of the club's boss, Frank. She had the bleach blonde hair and the Italian mob wife uniform of a fur coat and long acrylic nails. She had a motherly quality to her that I liked very much. I asked her if I would be taking clothes off- just wanted to double check that that would be what I would be doing. And she said, 'yes, dear- you're really green- I'll take you under my wing." After that I knew this would be the club best for me. We are still in contact after all these years and consider her to be a sort of mentor and good friend. Years later, I would later move on to other clubs, Scores NYC, Paradise Club Las Vegas and the Foxy Lady Providence, but Mario's always remained to be my 'home' club.

CHAPTER 2
SHOWTIME

The day after my 18th birthday, I went to work as an exotic dancer at the new club in Johnston, RI called Mario's Showplace ran by the couple, Frank and Marion. It was a brand-new club that hadn't opened yet and was still setting up.

The club had two stages- a main stage and a nude stage or 'The Nude Room', as it was called. As one of their main 'house girls' for nearly 7 years, I remained a loyal and valuable part of Mario's. A 'house girl' is a dancer who doesn't bounce around from club to club. Most girls would leave and come back, mostly due to stagnant income or unstable lifestyles or whatever reason. The 'house girls', which were only a handful of us, made sure the new girls followed the rules and called out any new dancers that tried to steal our clients. And by calling out, I mean, terrorizing them with itching powder in their costume bag (more on that later) and spreading unsavory rumors about them to get them fired. Hey, it was competitive to say the least and my priority was stay as the TOP bitch at the club.

I would have the stage to myself (no dancing partners) with a different themed-show nightly, especially on a weekend night. And I made the most money on a regular basis each night... so much so that my favorite bouncer, Gabe, would walk me to my car every night to keep other girls from jumping me. I had regular clients driving in from as far away as New Hampshire and Connecticut. 'TOP Bitch' was a hard title to defend, but I maintained it with my atrocious, intimidating behavior towards the other girls. As a matter of fact, new girls knew not to even give me eye contact or talk to me for at least a month. This was just my defense mechanism of weeding out the professional girls from the pedestrian hoes. Cutthroat was an understatement... Can you blame me?

CHAPTER 3
BITCHES

...And I don't mean that in an endearing way. In all my life, working in an environment that prizes your worth based on how you look is sure to bring out the worst in women. Hair-pulling, fistfights, conniving digs at each other, rumor spreading... all of it was just a part of the club atmosphere. The club was very strict on how their dancers should look... professionally done acrylic nails, no chipped toenails, long opera gloves and gown on the main stage (unless doing a themed show), a well-groomed who-ha (my signature was the late 90's Brazilian wax 'landing strip' or as some would call it, The Adolf), and absolutely no one pregnant or overweight. For the club's defense, there was a house girl who fell pregnant (the DJ was rumored to be the father)and no one had the heart to tell her to stop dancing... so she danced until she was 8 ½ months pregnant, which I must say is not very attractive in the scheme of things. Anyway, she popped the baby out and was back at work two weeks later. Amazing! The girls would take turns holding the baby in the dressing room while she was on stage.

The club would give out pink slips to anyone who gained weight (boob jobs were an exception) and the house mother would have you step on a scale once a week to prove it. This one time, I had just started birth control and it made my system all fucked and made me gain 10 lbs. It was awful! Thankfully, it ended up mostly in my boobs and I was able to stay at the club. In any case, this sort of 'competition' is surely to breed jealousy... throw in money and men... a total fucking shit show, a bloodbath, if you will. Actually, more like the high school cafeteria times 1,000.

While I started my dancing career, I was also going to Rhode Island College on full scholarship for Pre-Med/Biology, which I later changed a year into college to Communications/Public Relations. I just was not cut-out for the medical field. A creative free-spirit, I would rather write or make clothes than dissect a frog. Anyway, the word had gotten around somehow that I moonlit as an exotic dancer and while I bet most were intrigued, some would whisper and gossip about me all over campus. This created an uncomfortable atmosphere, which I learned to combat by surrounding myself with the misfits (who would later become fellow band members) and wonderfully unique people that I am proud to call my friends. They say college friends are your forever friends, which I agree wholeheartedly.

CHAPTER 4
BURLESQUE

Back in the mid '90s when Pamela Anderson, Carmen Electra and Jenna Jameson were at the top of their game, burlesque had exploded onto the scene and I was quick to jump in on it before it became mainstream with 'Lady Marmalade', etc. This was also when burlesque star Dita Von Teese was starting to gain traction and was touring American strip clubs. I have to say, it was wonderful to see Dita transform herself from fetish icon to the tame world of burlesque. Her shows at the time were still heavily fetish related, but she moved on to a more burlesque-y, fashion avenue, which she commands today worldwide. In a world of Jenna Jameson's and Pamela Anderson's, it was hard for a goth girl to maneuver the business like Dita, did.

And so, I looked to her career as a blueprint for myself, also a pale-skinned girl lost in a world of tanned beach bodies. Nonetheless, not only did I stand out of the bleach blonde, tanned crowd of strippers at the clubs, but I also perfected the art of making cash MONAY by befriending unhappily married, lonely, middle aged men. This was the secret to my success... look sophisticated and retro and listen to their mundane problems with a sweet demeanor. And maybe throw in some stand-up comedy along the way... that's it! While most dancers had occasional clients and a quick money mindset, I maintained a slick client portfolio of between 4-6 clients that spanned 5-7 years with a maintained cash flow every week. I was in it for the long haul- 8 years to be exact! And of course, there were the occasional clients that may not have stuck around because they were out of towners, bachelor parties, etc... they weren't regular strip club patrons, is what I mean.

So, I perfected my look with costumes found on my weekly trips to NYC with retro theme- fully-fashioned, nylon, thigh high stockings, six garter steel-boned corsets (all custom made in over 50 different fabrics) and a carefully curated playlist for every show. I was inspired by the Technicolor, old Hollywood look. I also chose the mysterious Russian stage name 'Tatiana'. It was marketing to the MAX, and I loved it!

The whole thing was kind of like acting, right? I knew if I invested my money wisely, I could possibly make enough to retire comfortably. Believe it or not, 25 years later, I'm still living off my dancing income. I was making as much as a surgeon for eight years straight- that's an average of $3500/week working 5 days a week. CASH! I was making so much money that I had to exchange everything into big bills and stash it in SEVERAL safe deposit boxes in undisclosed locations in Providence. I missed a lot of evening times with friends, boyfriends, and family. But with a salary like that, I couldn't say no. I was officially addicted to money. Is there such a thing? Abso-friggin-lutely. "Hey, Roxy, do you want to go see a band tonight?" – No, I'd rather make money. "Hey Roxy, do you want to have dinner with your visiting cousins?" No, I'll lose a ton of cash if I don't go in tonight.

It was so bad my addiction/obsession to work, that my boss ORDERED me to take a vacation every year... which I did, to the south of France with Troma (notice it's still a working vacation?) So, am I a workaholic or addicted to money? I think it's an unfortunate combination that if I didn't have some kind of intervention, I would've burned myself to the ground eventually. Which I did.... More on that later.

The collection of dancers the exotic dancing industry attracts ranges from quick-money, college girls (scale 1) to hard-core professional pornstars (scale 10). I'd like to say I was somewhere on the scale at a 7. I was taking this exotic dancing thing seriously, as a career, but not far enough to do porn. I wanted to definitely be financially independent and secure, with a house and car bought and paid for by age 25. I had a full scholarship for college, so that was not a burden. The only burden was making it to class in the mornings after getting home at 2am from work and financing my various auditions and headshots in NYC.

I had a very busy life that focused very much on career and little time on serious dating. I was making more than my broke college friends and it placed an awkwardness when planning outings and stuff. I wanted to go to The Capital Grille for dinner, but they could only afford Taco Bell. I got tired of footing the bill for everyone all the time and began to doubt my friends' authenticity. So, I decided to focus on work and a bit of dating....

The thing about having older men in your company all the time is that you learn to smell the bullshit of young men fairly quickly. Why should I date a guy that makes less money than me and tells me what I can and can't do? Fuck that noise! I'd say most of the guys I dated, after a few months they would ask me to quit my dancing job because they didn't like other guys looking at me. Total bullshit, because they were attracted to me because of my very exciting 'executive' job, yet most were unable to support me financially because they were too busy smoking pot and planning the next local rave. So, most of the guys I ended up dating were merely boy toys to pass the time and amuse me, as harsh as that sounds.

I had bigger fish to fry... like getting a sugar daddy to buy me a brand-new BMW 7 series, paying off a mortgage on my house and first class trips around the world . Hustling became my craft. And my final scheme that didn't pan out? Acquiring an apartment in NYC under my name and starring in a sugar daddy- financed feature film, which would lead me to the introduction of my future husband. Hahaha... funny how life works!

Enjoy this collection of random little stories and bigger stories about my double life as an actress and exotic dancer all intertwined, like the roots of a tree... crossing and weaving with purpose and direction, yet still forming a solid base for the person I have become today.

CHAPTER 5
CLIENTS

I have to say, the hardest part about being an exotic dancer is not dealing with the men…. It was dealing with co-workers. Jealousy, rivalry and betrayal was pretty standard. Girls would do anything to 'steal' a client, whether it was spreading a nasty rumor about the dancer or just mentioning that the dancer had a 'serious boyfriend'. This way, in the client's mind, there would never be a chance of 'getting' the girl.

It was all really a game… appear interested in what the client has to say and share, swindle him to spend 'time' with you- preferably in the 'Champagne Room' where girls would command up to $350/ hour (champagne not included, of course) , and then basically be a hot, sexy shrink that lap dances sporadically, while the client tells you every detail of their fucked up life. Hopefully, that will take a few hours because, remember, you're being paid hourly or by the song. After, cleaning out the dude's wallet, wish the guy a splendid week and hope to see him again and make sure to rattle off your work schedule before he leaves the club. Rinse and repeat.

Very rarely did I have a problem with a man not paying for my time. I had a diplomatic way of doing business, though. I would never ask for money upfront. I would let the guy initiate payment, unless I got a sneaky vibe from the person, to which I would ask for payment at the end of each song. Champagne Room was a totally different beast… payment was upfront when buying the champagne with the house, so I would say, 'Let's take care of business first, while we're at it.' Sometimes, I would say the house required me to take payment upfront. This way, there was no awkwardness or possibility of getting stiffed (PUN, intended).

    That business flow was ideal for the kinds of clients that the club would attract- mostly bored husbands working mundane jobs as lawyers, doctors, accountants, judges, 'construction' business, and occasionally a certain mayor ...you get the drift. Men were not the only club patrons. I had a handful of lesbian women and couples as clients over the years. Dancing for a lesbian is exactly the same as dancing for a guy, believe it not.... Maybe a little bit more sensual, but everything else- same.

    Occasionally, I would get men with strange fetishes, like tickling or this one dude that wanted me to spit on him repeatedly. I'll never forgot this one guy that claimed his wife had 'hypnotized' him to give her money by putting her hand on her left hip and said 'purchase', he would give her $100 dollars. I tried it just for laughs. That night, I made $1500 in just under 20 minutes. You can imagine the contained excitement I felt, just enough not to tip off the other girls abut my gold mine ! He came in several times after that in a span of 6 months. I bet his wife 'un-hypnotized' after seeing his bank statements. Most of my fetish clients had standard preferences like stockings, garters, corsets, you know, usual stuff that men go wild on and that most women find to be a pain in the ass to wear. Luckily, I found it all very amusing to wear.

CHAPTER 6
THE JAPANESE BUSINESSMEN

I had several Japanese clients over the years. They all shared a common thread of being very respectful, incredibly polite and OUTRAGEOUSLY generous. There was one Japanese client, Yori, that would bring his business associates on every visit every month.

Rhode Island has a fabric manufacturing industry, as well as the headquarters for Swarovski crystals. Yori was in town to broker a deal with his clients and the way to celebrate and seal the deal was with booze and hot, naked chicks, naturally. Being the late nineties and early 2000s, being tan was in and nearly every dancer in the club was a nice shade in between of beef jerky and a Louis Vuitton bag. The Japanese have a preference for pale-skinned chicks, so I nailed that niche single-handedly in our club.

Fun Fact: before I became an exotic dancer fresh out of high school, I explored the idea of becoming a Geisha in Kyoto. I had read 'Memoirs of a Geisha' a million times and researched it in depth, finally deciding that it would take too many years as a Maiko (geisha in training) in a foreign land that I don't speak the language. So that idea was squashed.

Back to the story, there were maybe four to five Japanese businessmen at a time wheeling and dealing in Japanese and then there was little old me sitting with a Shirley Temple waiting for them to loosen up and get some private lap dances. Enticing them with the champagne room was not a choice because they didn't want to be impolite and abandon their business associates for hours. So, I would take turns with each of them for private dances, since they would politely decline dances from all the other tanned dancers. I would also really play it up with several silk custom-made corseted Geisha costumes. They loved it! I bet they felt like they were samurais in Gion or something. Okay, maybe they felt it was more like an X-rated Benihana minus the food.

I was pretty much booked for the entire night with my Japanese clients. Sometimes they would just want me to sit and have a drink with them and practice their English and me, practice Japanese. Sometimes I would dance for them and put on little Geisha –themed shows on stage for them. Sometimes I would give them a proper lap dance and make them blush, actually it was probably the alcohol making them blush. Anyway, in any case, I knew I was set for the night money-wise when they would come in. Yori would pay me a cool $1,00 for the entire night with his associates and occasionally would come in alone to see me.

One night, he came in alone and told me he was moving back to Japan. BUMMER! On top of being very generous during all those years, he was truly a cool guy. He barely spoke English, but his manners were beyond anything I had experienced in the club…. A true gentleman. We exchanged emails and wished each other well. Years later, my husband and I spent our honeymoon in Japan. One leg of the trip was in the Gion district of Kyoto…. Sometimes I wonder what if I had become a Geisha and what ever happened to Yori? I hope he's somewhere in the world making million dollar deals with a fine-aged sake in hand surrounded by gorgeous Geishas!

CHAPTER 7
NERDY ENGAGEMENT

One of my clients for a short time was a car mechanic that still lived with his aging parents. It was sort of unusual because he was a relatively attractive man that had a good job, perfectly capable of starting his own life with his own place and possibly a girlfriend, yet he refused to take that leap for whatever reason. Now, I'm not a shrink, but I think he suffered from severe self-esteem issues. The guy was thinly built of average height with a buzzcut and had a nerdy demeanor about him. He preferred to drink club soda, rather than alcohol like his buddies.

He and his work buddies would come in every Friday night and drop some significant cash... at least for a car mechanic. This lasted a few months. I was his favorite and soon he began to come in without his buddies during the week. He told me that he was a virgin.... Like a real-life 30-year-old virgin. I don't know where he was getting all this cash, but I knew he was definitely saving his pennies to see me at the club. In a way, I felt bad that he had never experienced a proper fuck, but in a business way I thought 'not my problem, just take the cash'.

The following Friday night, he came in with his buddies. This time I felt he was nervous and bashful more than usual. What was up?... I wondered... one of his buddies told another dancer that he had bought an engagement ring and was planning on proposing to me that night. Ever hear of a cockblock? Well, let's call this a PUSSY block! The dancer told my client not to give me the ring because I had a boyfriend and I would say no. First of all, don't get up in my business, bitch! And second of all, yes, I had a boyfriend, but I would've taken the ring and kindly said no. I know, looking back, that would have been totally shitty of me to do, but business is business, right?

So, my nerdy client ran out of the club before he could even ask me, and before I could even say hello and talk to him. One of his buddies them proceeded to tell me he was going to propose and that how he was in debt with all his visits to me at the club. Some people have a gambling problem and some people have a pussy problem... he had a pussy problem. Not my problem, but I still felt bad about it all. I never saw him again and I blacklisted the beeotch who Pussy Blocked me. I truly hope he has found happiness with a woman that matches him and appreciates him.... and that he gets his chest waxed occasionally while screaming, "KELLY CLARKSON!

CHAPTER 8
JACK THE EYE DOCTOR

It was a rainy day and the club was super dead. I had picked up day shifts in the beginning of my dancing career because I still had to keep my job incognito. So, the easy 11am-6pm day shift was the perfect cover for, say, a waitressing job at 'The Ground Round'. (*side note: The Ground Round was like a fine dining establishment for hillbillies. Probably in the Chili's range, but less TexMex.*) I had already been dancing for about six months, when a tall man with glasses, toupee and a suit walked in. Bingo! A balding businessman on his lunch break... perfect! You can always tell a guy coming in on his lunch break... sort of in a rush, minimal conversation, doesn't care about getting a drink, but scans the room for a hot chick to take in the back straight away. Being the ATM 'guard', I would spot these kinds of guys as soon as they walked in. These types of clients were my favorite, especially on a boring day shift.

Jack was one of these clients. I didn't really start talking to him until he realized the he should probably wait for the downpour to clear. He worked as a doctor about 20 minutes away at a chain eyeglasses store in the mall. So, after a few lap dances, he invited me to sit with him and have a drink until the weather cleared. Seeing the club was pretty much empty and all the day-shift girls, mostly single moms lamenting about their deadbeat baby daddies, were gathered in a corner day drinking, I took him up on his offer. He was a charming man in a geeky way. We talked about everything... his frigid Japanese wife, his two children in junior high school... his wealthy in-laws, how his business was thriving at a record pace.... all of it.

And I gave him my usual story of struggling college student working as a stripper to pay off school tuition and get into acting. The rain had let up and it was time for him to go... after that he would come in regularly twice a week to see me. He would spend about 45 minutes at the club and I would make $200 each visit. He had now become a regular client of mine.

After about a year, I had stopped working day shifts and started working evening shifts only. So, he would visit early during my shift after he got off work at 5:30pm before going home. It was during this time that he proposed to meet me for lunch outside the club. I agreed and decided to meet him at a restaurant at another mall. It went well and did a little shopping with him and decided it's ok to do this as a regular thing, seeing he is not a stalker/serial killer type.

Usually, men with wives and children are a good target for sugar daddy potential, because they have too much to lose, if caught. So, he would give me $400/week in the club plus a lunch date and shopping spree every week. Wednesdays were our lunch and shopping days, usually. At the time, BEBE, Nordstrom, BCBG were my favorite stores in that particular mall. Sometimes, I would meet him in Boston on Newbury Street and do lunch and shopping there. He would end up buying me about $300-500 worth of stuff every week. Fur coats, evening gowns, shoes, handbags, jewelry... you name it. My wardrobe was mainly sponsored by this man... many of which I still have today in my closet. He even ended up buying most of my custom corsets and costumes throughout the years... each one costing an upwards of $800.

This arrangement lasted about seven years... right up until my retirement at age 25.

There was a small break about six years in... apparently, the wife had found a diamond ring meant for me in his glove compartment one day. The wife confronted Jack and he said it was a surprise for her! Ha! The wife grew suspicious, I guess he wasn't exactly the type to buy expensive jewelry on a whim for his wife, so she hired a private detective and saw photos from our outings and found out about our arrangement.

One morning, I was expecting a phone call from a casting agent. The phone rang and I answered excitedly... except, it was Jack's angry wife! I could barely understand her, but I did get "noooo expensive gift for you!". To which I freaked out and hung up! My brain still confused and racked, a few minutes later, Jack calls me to tell me she knows and that he has to take a break from seeing me for a little while. I felt bad more for Jack than the wife. I don't like getting into people's business about why they are 'unfaithful', even just emotionally unfaithful. But it happens more often than you think.

Is it really cheating, if there is no physical relationship? Some people say yes, others say no. I'd like to think no... and that's because I feel society puts pressure on people to be one person's *everything*. Maybe we were meant to have several close people in our lives... one for sexual relationships, one for meaningful, deep conversations, one to vent to when we have a shitty day, and one to take care of the family home and children... you know several networks of partners to keep life fulfilled. I don't think there's anything wrong with that. I feel it just puts high expectations on a relationship that is not capable of reciprocating all the facets a person requires to live a fulfilled life. Maybe it's just my bullshit excuse to gather as many sugar daddies for myself... I dunno.

So, Jack did come back after a couple of months, but I had already been staging my exit from the exotic dancing scene... I was approaching 25 and was growing tired of the business. I did see Jack a handful of times after, mainly to pass me a cash filled envelope to maintain my lifestyle, but those soon ended, as did our sugar daddy/sugar baby relationship. After all, I had bigger conquests... Tim, as you will read next ...

CHAPTER 9
POUR SOME SUGAR ON ME

There comes a time in a dancer's career where one client becomes the sole 'sponsor' of the dancer. The client falls a little too hard, so much so that it ends up being a sugar daddy/sugar baby situation. This is any gold digger/ exotic dancers dream! As a matter of fact, this is the type of situation that is highly coveted and difficult to achieve without actually physical sex. So, if you are able to swindle a sugar daddy without sleeping with him, you deserve a goddamn award! I must say, I deserve that goddamn award myself because the day that Tim walked into my life, the gold digger angels were singing to high heaven. He was my lord and savior and I didn't even know it until a full six months into having him as a client.

Tim was a middle aged, heavyset man that owned an eyeglasses factory. He was married with two children. I didn't find all this out until maybe four months into seeing him. The first four months, he was a very quiet guy that chose me every time for a private dance. He would visit the club weekly and had a penchant for my shows, which included a rubber nurse costume, geisha costumes, latex military costume, boxer costume, French maid with stockings and garters, various Burlesque corsets and stockings, angel wings, Barbie, you name it. I think I even had a prisoner/jailbait costume with my measurements as my prison numbers displayed on my chest. Anyway, I loved coming up with different costumes and shows. It was all part of the fun.

Being in demand, I thought I should see if he wants to book me for champagne rooms instead. He was coming in spending an hour or two at the club, waiting half the time while I went on stage, etc. and spending the same amount of money. Might as well book me for a solid hour or two for himself, for the same price, right? Well, during these champagne room rendezvous, we got to talk intimately without interruption. I soon found he was in an unhappy marriage and was going through a nasty divorce and custody battle. He was also battling with being obese.

After a few months of weekly champagne room giving advice, he announced his divorce was final and that he had reached an agreement in the custody battle. Not only that, he was in the middle of negotiations to sell his successful eyeglasses factory (who made Elton John prescription sunglasses when he was on a trip in Martha's Vineyard) to a French company for a cool seven figures. We celebrated, naturally, with champagne and toasted to a new beginning. I encouraged Tim to hire a personal trainer/nutrition adviser and that I would become his personal fashion stylist. He was down for it all and so our special friendship/sponsor or sugar daddy/sugar baby relationship began lasting until even after I retired from dancing... a full eight years.

Tim would come in weekly to see me, booking me for the last four hours of the night on a Saturday night for a cool $1500. And that was just my fee... not including alcohol, food, house fees and waitress tips. He would take interest in what I was doing in college, making sure I got good grades, etc. Our relationship had passed the sexual fantasy stage and had taken on the role of concerned 'father' and college-aged daughter role. It was exactly what I need at the time, since I had become estranged from my father during my college years. And I was exactly what Tim needed at the time, a friend to lend an ear and teach him about the luxuries of life and how to a spend that newly acquired CASH MONAY.

After a while, I wouldn't even dance for him. He would ask me to stay fully clothed all night and just have conversations with me. As I began to trust him, I would meet him for lunch at various upscale restaurants in Providence. I would always take my own car and meet him in public. Soon, we would do lunch and shopping in Boston and NYC... at Chanel, Bergdorf's, Barney's, and Neiman's. Shopping for me, but also for him... I would style designer outfits for him and be his personal shopper.

Tim was living the life as a newly minted millionaire and was starting to look and act the part, thanks to me. He had lost a total of 150 lbs and was gaining his confidence back in a real way. Long gone was the timid, overweight man battling depression. We were happy with our arrangement and that's all that mattered.

Over the years, he would book me for every single Saturday night and would start bringing in two of his buddies. I would get my usual $1500 fee. I also was in charge of choosing any two dancer friends (many of whom tried to steal my client in deceitful ways, but never succeeded) to join his friends in the champagne room. So, this translated to all the girls kissing my lily-white ass all week to get me to choose them to make $1000 that Saturday night. It was hilarious. I had decided that whoever I choose, I get a 20% cut of that $1000 from EACH dancer that night. That's an extra $400 every Saturday night for doing ABSOLUTELY nothing. If that ain't pimping, I don't know what is. So, I would pull in an easy $2,000 every Saturday night for about 4 years straight.... And I wouldn't even have to take my clothes off anymore. FUCKING BRILLIANT.

So, I thought let's take this a step further. My car was old 328i BMW from like 1985. I think the only reason I would drive it was because it was the color of that hot Chanel nail polish, VAMP. Any who, I wanted a new car and Tim the sugar daddy was gonna pay for it. Now, I had heard stories of clients buying their dancer friends brand new cars with a loan still attached and the title in the name of said sugar daddy, only to have it repossessed when things didn't go sugar daddy's way. So, I thought I should get a used car with low mileage and have it paid outright in cash with the title in my name. Tim was really hellbent on going to the BMW dealer and getting me a brand new 5 series, but I wasn't going to fall into that unfortunate, failed, gold digger situation of having my car repossessed a few years later. So, I explained to him how the value of a car drops when you drive it off the lot, etc etc.... you know hustling him like I was a keen businesswoman and stuff.

One week later, we went over to Massachusetts and picked up a black, 1995 740il BMW with low mileage and for sure was a body bag transport car for the Mafia in another lifetime. How it all went down was fast, efficient and brilliant. We saw the car at the used dealership, I looked inside, I looked outside and said 'this is the one'. Tim was like, 'ummm ok.... Don't you want to see other stuff?' and I was like, 'nope'. I wanted to seal the deal fast before he changed his mind.

So, we go into the used car dealership office. The sleazy car salesman probably was catching on to the extent our relationship and asked immediately whose name should go under the title. I waited for

Tim to respond, to which he responded… 'Under her name only'. HALLELUJAH!! I didn't even have to bullshit that one! The next question was if we needed a loan. I nervously glanced over to Tim and he responded immediately, 'Nope. All cash." At that point, I almost shat my pants. The car was going to be in my name with no loan! The car, brand new, at the time was worth $90,000. This was a few years old, used, so Tim paid $45,000 cash right there in that dude's office. When you start counting $45,000 worth of cash in a used car salesman's office who may or may not moonlight as a loanshark a) it starts to get awkward after counting past $10,000 b)You hurry the fuck up and wrap up the deal before any 'associates' come in to rob you in the office.

So, after a solid 45 minutes of counting cash and signing papers, the car was mine and ready to be driven off the lot home. Right, so, I was pretty good at hiding expensive gifts and cash from my mom and brother (whom I was still living with), but what the fuck was I going to say about flashy, drug dealer's car worth $90,000 acquired a few days before Valentine's Day?? All I remember was driving off the lot worried. Worried that Tim might have a buyer's remorse and make me return it and get his money back and worried about how I'm going to explain this to my family, who still did not know I was an exotic dancer after all of the years. They thought I was just a waitress in a bar.

I sped past Tim in my new car and headed home. The feeling of excitement, accomplishment and anxiety was overwhelming me. I had decided to come clean to my family. I was going to tell them I have a rich suitor that I met at the bar. That's it. I wasn't going to reveal anything about being an exotic dancer. Just some dude who goes to the bar that wanted to buy me a car. That's all.

I pull up at home and my BMW fan of a brother is already coming out to see the car. Shit! I haven't even gotten out of the car, yet! So, that day, I sat my mom and brother down and explained the 'rich suitor' and just waitressing at a bar. Whew! They bought the story, for now.

After Tim had bought me the car, I could feel he was getting a little anxious. I was beginning to wonder if he was growing tired of our sugar daddy/sugar baby set up. That's when I suggested we go on a trip. I had always wanted to travel to England and why not on someone else's dime? Tim had never been to Europe, so it was the perfect excuse to go celebrate with his millions. At this point, I was pretty comfortable with him. I would allow him to drive me in his new Porsche 911 to NYC and Boston and felt like we had passed the serial killer/ax murderer stage of our friendship. I do want to re-iterate that I had never had any sexual relations with him at any point, besides just lap dancing at the club. He clearly respected me and didn't expect anything from me. Honestly, he just wanted to make sure I got good grades in college and stayed away from drugs, very fatherly and friendly.

So, he booked us two round-trip First-class tickets to London staying for a total of 10 days at The Ritz Hotel, not to be confused with The Ritz-Carlton, which is not as ritzy as The Ritz in London, if you can believe it. The Ritz is a super-exclusive hotel right around the corner from Buckingham Palace. It is so exclusive, that you have a view of the Queen's backyard from the rooms. As a matter of fact, it is rumored the suite I stayed in was the same suite that a member of the Iranian Royal family (that was apparently living there long-term) overdosed and died.

Tim had booked a two-room suite with its own private butler outside of our door. The rooms were in a lush pink Victorian design, very Marie Antoinette, but British... if that makes any sense. Our keys were actually old-fashioned skeleton keys that we would have to turn in to the concierge every time we left the hotel. No credit card door keys here! Our stay was magnificent! I had planned our entire trip... a train ride to Cambridge to visit Oxford University, another train ride to Brussels, Belgium for the day, exploring the London Tower and other touristic sites, and shopping in Camden-Locke and Piccadilly Circus. We had high tea at The Savoy; breakfast every morning at The Ritz restaurant, and lavish dinners at some of the most exclusive restaurants in London.

One night we met a few of my British friends and partied all night in our suite. During our visit, I had appointments for fittings and shopping at several latex and corset boutiques, including the *House of Harlot*. There I picked up several custom costumes that I had pre-ordered by phone weeks prior and a few corsets. It was nice to meet the people who actually made my costumes... everything was over the phone and fax, still.

Speaking of phones, every night I would pick up my hotel room phone and call my mom and my best friend Melanie in the US and talk for hours. I had no clue that this was going to be expensive until Tim got the bill upon check out. I may or may not have ordered room services nightly.... Ok yes, a little ice cream and fruit, maybe.... Ok, maybe a filet mignon with 'chips'? Anyway, upon check out, I could tell Tim was trying to contain his disbelief when he got the bill. He never got mad at me directly, but I could tell he was pissed...considering our last night, he tried to kiss me on the lips, which I dodged coyly and retired to my suite.

I could feel the end of his sponsorship was near and he was losing his patience with me.

    Back to the bill, apparently my calls alone cost $10,000. Ha! Insane! In my defense, it was my first time staying in a really nice hotel and had no idea of extra charges like that. I thought the calls would be free, like already included with our outrageously priced suites. The flight back was awkward and long. We didn't really speak, and we were coincidentally flying back on the same plane as my mom's friend. I had to awkwardly lie and say that Tim was a film director friend of mine and we were location scouting. I mean, I couldn't say he was a family member, because the guy knew my family already and Tim looked more like a Scandinavian dude than a Persian guy. It was a memorable trip and it opened my eyes to a whole new world besides the dark, dingy nightclub. Our arrangement lasted longer than I thought after that… well after I retired from dancing, and led me to the introduction of my future husband.

CHAPTER 10
MAKE IT PURPLE RAIN

One of my first regular clients was a thinly built, 30 something, Hispanic man that had a fascination with Prince. We'll call him Purple Rain. I must've only been dancing for a few weeks when I had met him during the day shift. We would be able to choose the music we danced to, as long as we tipped the DJ generously. My choice of music happened to be coincidentally, Prince. I'm a big Prince fan, but not as much as this guy. This guy was FAN. AT. TI. CAL. I think I was dancing to "7" by Prince wearing a belly dancer type outfit with my hair done like Mayte Garcia complete with a sculpted pin curl at the top of my forehead, when Purple Rain approached the stage with mesmerized eyes. It was the first time I had seen a guy so mesmerized by me! Or maybe it was just the Prince song. Any who, he started tipping me on stage with $20s and $10s … then he ran out and started tipping me with $50 bills. He asked me to join him for a drink after my set. The set ended, got dressed and joined him and his friend, a muscular tall man who seemed uninterested in anything that came his way.

Purple Rain was a shy, laid back, smooth-talking type of guy… kind of what I would imagine Prince to have been in real life! We had interesting banter, mostly revolving around how much he loved Prince and that he loved that I had dressed like Mayte for my set with the song '7'. I wanted to tell him, yes, it's called a 'show', but I went with it and got another $300 out of him for just sitting with him. He wasn't really interested in me dancing privately for him, I think he just wanted the company more than anything. I mean, his friend barely talked and was not engaging in any kind of conversation or anything. I got the vibe his friend was more a 'bodyguard' more than anything... like he was paid to be there.

The next month would involve me dancing to various Prince songs and wearing purple costumes and what not to when Purple Rain would visit and making about $500 each time. He always had a thick roll of cash with him on every visit. I'm talking big bills... $20s, $50s, $100s. So, after a month of Purple Rain coming to see me weekly during the day shift, he asked me if I would go out to dinner and a nightclub with him. I agreed, mainly because he seemed pretty harmless and gentle and he was pretty fun to talk to as long as I was prepared to hear about the 'Purple One' for hours on end. Also, I had planned on going with my sometimes dance partner, Ocean. Ocean was a beautiful, black woman with the body of Naomi Campbell. She was GORGEOUS and one of my best work friends. She always joked how "she was a white woman trapped in a black woman's body". Ocean also had a penchant for dating handsome Italian guys. We would match our outfits together on stage... we were literally, like Ebony and Ivory. I remember we had matching costumes with the caged pants and top- she had white; I had a black version. We would only dance to Prince's music on the main stage.

She agreed to come along with his bodyguard friend, who serendipitously, was a handsome Italian guy. We met at an Italian restaurant called "The Florentine Grill" just outside of Providence. It was one of the fine dining restaurants that attracted the small-town mafia crowd. Small town mafia crowd, as in not the head boss, but the minions of the head bosses. We had a lovely dinner, despite talking my ear off about Prince and were ready to go to a nightclub. We all packed into his Denali and went to a club in Providence.

Okay, South Providence is a pretty rough neighborhood... and I never go there unless a) I had to drop off that one dancer (more on that later or b) if I had to go the hospital, which Rhode Island Hospital is located (ideally or not ideally- depends on how you look at it).

I was a bit freaked out until, Purple Rain walked in the club knowing every single damn person in there. Quiet, muscular bodyguard was right behind us and we walk into a roped off VIP area. This place was no Avalon- Boston, but it was no shack either. It dawned on me that he might be a small-time drug dealer. Whatever, it was a fun night and Purple Rain was every bit a gentleman. At the end of the night, his friend and him drop Ocean and I off at my car back at the Florentine Grill and he made plans immediately to see me at the club later that week. He continued to come in on a regular basis for a few months after that with a couple more outings to dinner. Then, he stopped coming in all of a sudden. I really didn't think nothing of it, I thought the guy is busy and I didn't want to seem like I was hounding him for money. Remember I was still new at the game.

A couple weeks pass, and he finally shows up at the club.... Pissed. He asked me why I didn't contact him to see how he was, etc. I had no real answer for him. It was clear he was thinking I was his girlfriend, when I viewed it as a business arrangement. I mean, we had never even kissed! He clearly was heartbroken, and I felt awful, but realized this was bound to happen. Although it was not my intention to hurt him, I had, and I felt a bit of remorse. I apologized and that was the last time I saw Purple Rain. I knew that from then on, I shouldn't feel bad for the bad choices others make. I thank Purple Rain for teaching me how to navigate the waters without feeling guilty. And every time I hear 'Erotic City', I think of that shy, generous, laid-back gentleman with the rolls of cash!

CHAPTER 11
WHITEY THE LAWYER

One day I noticed an older gentleman with a full head of perfectly, white hair and tailored suit visit the club. I had seen him before at the club with other girls, so I never bothered to introduce myself. I didn't want to step on anybody's toes. Well, his regular gaggle of ladies were not there, and he seemed to be alone for a little while. So, I decided to swoop in and see what his story was about. Lucky for me, he was on the prowl for a new girl and I just happened to be at the right time and place. We will call him Whitey, for his marvelous hair.

He was a fun-loving gentleman brimming with lawyer jokes. I gathered he was a criminal lawyer, but I didn't realize how much of an influential Providence lawyer he was until he started telling me stories about some of his cases. Like the one where he knew the judge from high school and got a formerly convicted drug dealer off. Apparently, the guy had a suitcase full of cocaine in his trunk and lucky him, Whitey had gotten him off completely... not even a plea deal. The man walked out of the courtroom and that was that. He had other stories, too, but it didn't matter to me... what was clear was that Whitey was LOADED and I wanted, not only a piece of the pie,... I wanted to be on his PAYROLL. We shared some laughs and he invited to spend the rest of the night in the Champagne Room.

He ended up becoming a regular client for about a year before he moved on to another girl. It was a miracle already that I could hold his attention for a full year. He would visit the club regularly (about one weekday night) and book me for the Champagne Room every time. He would arrive later in the night (around 11pm) and close out the night with me, which was great, because I could just sit back and relax the last couple hours of the night. We would make jokes, tell each other stories of the week and of course, I would dance for him. We engaged in naughty banter, but he never crossed the line of being disrespectful. That's what I liked about him, his old school manners. Anyway, I knew he was the type of guy that gets bored easily, and likes variety, so I would prepare myself for the brush off every time I would see him.

One night, I was surprised to hear him ask me out to dinner outside of the club. Normally, I wouldn't accept, but seeing that I actually liked his company and he was such an influential man in Providence, I accepted. A few nights later, I met him at a fine Italian restaurant in Providence called Capriccio's. Capriccio's is the type of restaurant that not only requires reservations, but also a bulletproof vest. The place is the type of establishment where the Mafia drink Chianti, converse, wheel and deal; eat risotto de arancini all the while plotting the murdering of their non-suspecting associates. It's the kind of place where you sit with your back to the wall, in case, you know, something happens. The place has tiles floors for a reason, quick clean-ups. Nonetheless, I was beyond excited. I had gotten my nails and hair done and picked out the perfect mafia 'girlfriend' dress.

As soon as I walked in, they took my fur coat and seated me with NOT my back to the wall…. It was going to be an interesting evening of looking over my shoulder all night. Whitey did bring me flowers, so that was a good sign that he didn't want to kill me for knowing too much. After all, I didn't want to end up like the poor stripper who had her nipples cut off and set on fire in a bathtub a few months prior. Police, conveniently, never 'solved' the case and it had minimal news coverage.

Unsurprisingly, the staff knew Whitey very well, which would only confirm his status of possibly, probably lawyer to the mafia. After a lovely five course Italian gourmet meal, we decided to have a night cap around the corner at a neighborhood Italian bar, where he knew everyone, as well. I was pleasantly surprised that he didn't try anything on me at the end of the night. He 'took care' of the valet for my car and sent me on my merry way with a sweet kiss on the cheek. I felt every bit the part of 'mafia girlfriend' that night, minus the FBI wire and guns.

Our 'relationship' would last in and out of the club for another 10 months. He even got me out of a speeding ticket. He took my ticket and POOF!... no court date, no fine, no record. After our business relationship had ended, I would still see him in the club as he had moved on to other girls, as expected. But we would always greet each other warmly and exchange cheeky banter for a quick minute. Years later, I ran into Whitey at the courthouse with his toothy grin and white, billowy hair. He winked at me from afar as the judge's gavel fell and his client gave him a hearty hug. I'm telling you, it had to be the hair!

CHAPTER 12

STALKING STATE TROOPER

Usually, I would avoid the policemen, firemen, etc. at the club. Only because I felt they probably didn't have enough money for a long-term arrangement. I was looking for more the rich dude with disposable income to put me on the 'payroll', indefinitely.

A couple of Rhode Island State Troopers walked in one night. They were not in their uniforms and were off-duty, but they were all drinking Coors Lights, which was a dead giveaway for a cop... or at least a hard clue. One guy, a well-built man with a sandy blonde buzzcut took an interest with me. He paid for some lap dances and didn't talk much. I always preferred not talking much if the client wasn't inclined to make conversation. I didn't want to ruin the 'fantasy' by prying and asking small-talk questions. He was polite, exact and reserved. I could tell he had military training by his manners and disposition. He asked me when I would be working next and promised to see me again.

The following week, he came into the club alone and spent about an hour with me. He didn't have any weird fetishes or preferences. This time he asked me questions of where I go to school and what town I'm from. I always had a bullshit story ready to divert any strange stalkers. Our club at trained us to come up with a bullshit backstory to protect our safety and privacy. My bullshit backstory was that I was studying pre-med at Brown University (bullshit) and that I danced to pay my way through college (true true). My real name is actually my stage name, Tatiana (bullshit). I live on the East Side of Providence with a few college friends (bullshit). I have three Persian cats (true true). Any other detail questions I would just make up on the fly. I guess it was improv for all us theater people.

So, I gave him my bullshit story, which obviously he didn't buy. In any case, he seemed to be a calculating man, yet very, very polite. He asked me if I could see him outside of the club. I gave him a firm no. I knew that meeting a cop outside of the club could very well be a trap, plus I didn't feel comfortable enough to see him outside the club. There was something 'off' about him. Not only that, but he was probably the type to forgo the financial portion of our arrangement as soon as he would see me outside the club. The guy was just looking for a girlfriend. He didn't take my answer very well, ... but he persisted on the next two visits. He asked me one last time on his last visit if I would meet him outside the club...I stuck to my guns and said no.... He left, no hard feelings. And that was that.

A few days later, I was driving around near my house running errands when a state trooper's lights go off behind me. I was driving super slow, my taillights were fine, what could I have possibly done? I pull over and wait. A dark shadow of a man comes up and it's HIM, the State Trooper! As he gets closer, I see a big grin on his face. Oh shit! It could go either way... either he takes out his frustration on me and gives me a big fat ticket OR he lets me go. He says, 'I knew it was you!' So, I greeted him and asked him if I did anything wrong. He said matter-of-factly, that he had pulled me over to ask me out. I was partly relieved and partly livid. This was going to be a touchy situation given the fact that the dude can throw me in jail for pretty much anything.... I mean, do you think a judge would believe a decorated State Trooper or a stripper???

Long story short... I was fucked. I really didn't want to go out with this guy, honestly, he sort of freaked me with his reserved , yet calculating behavior and he had stopped spending money with me, so the answer was still going to be no. I didn't dare to ask him if it was a coincidence that he saw my car or that he ran my plates. I told him he can see me at the club later that night. He let me go and said he would drop by after work. Later that night, he came in and didn't stay for long, just enough for one drink and one dance. He asked me out AGAIN. I said it's against club rules, blah blah blah. He left agitated. I thought nothing of it and went about the rest of my night.

A few days later, I was at home with my mother, when his State Trooper car pulled up in our driveway. My mother saw from the window and told me there's a cop in the driveway. Freaked out quietly, I calmly told her, it's a friend and to not worry... I go out and greet him before he can came out of his car. The first thing he said to me was, 'Is that a stuffed animal in your window?', referring to my plump, white Persian cat, Mr. MarMar, who was staring out of the window suspiciously at the man. Mr. Marmar probably sensed a no-good situation... or maybe he just had an excellent spot in the sun, I dunno. I thought to myself, this motherfucker ran my plates to find where I live! I told him that I lived with my mom and that she didn't know about my dancing career and that he had freaked her out by coming into our driveway. He found it all very amusing. I found it to be irritating and stressful. His words were, 'So, are you gonna go out on a date with me or what?'. I mulled it over for a second or two thinking maybe I can get rid of him if I say yes, and responded, NO and to just please see me at the club, like I had asked. I thought this was the kind of man that would keep harassing me to get his way and I wasn't about to have that. He said fine and that he'll be back. I left and went back inside and made up a bullshit story or my mom about how I know a State Trooper. She probably didn't believe me, but I was off the hook for now- from both my mom and State Trooper.

Late afternoon the next day while driving to work, guess who pulls me over? This time, I was PISSED. This time, he demanded 'Go out on a date with me.' I say no and that I have to go to work, I'm running late. He then threatened to arrest me for 'soliciting', if I didn't 'cooperate'. Not only was I pissed, but a little scared because this guy could say ANYTHING, and people would believe him over me just because he had a badge. A classic case of misuse of power. So, I looked at his badge and memorized the number. I responded that I knew his badge number and that I would report him if he keeps harassing me. It was a long shot in getting him to back off, hell, the plan might have backfired in my face. I politely said, "Please leave me alone and started my engine and drove away. I hurried over to the club and ran into the office to find my boss, Frank. I was already late for work, which was highly unusual. The only other time I was ever late for work was when my boyfriend at the time decided to have 'make-up' sex a few days after one Thanksgiving weekend. We had broken up for about two weeks and missed each other immensely. THAT was worth being late for work for, but this? Fuck that shit!

I told Frank everything that had transpired during the last two months. Frank asked me for his badge number and name. He wrote it down and gave it to one of his sons. Frank told me not to worry and that he would 'take care of it'. I felt relieved that I could tell someone about the situation. It's not like I could tell just anyone, especially my family.

Well, I NEVER saw State Trooper again! Rhode Island is a small state where everyone runs into each other and knows everyone. I never ran into this guy ever again. My boss really did 'take care of it' and I don't want to know how! Thank you, Frank!

CHAPTER 13

VIVIANA AND THE CASE OF THE ITCHING POWDER

A few of my girlfriends shared a dorm with another girl that apparently was slightly obsessed about me. I would visit my friends' dorm once in a while and didn't really pay attention to this girl. Her name was Anne. A petite girl of Puerto Rican descent with nondescript features. Basically, if I saw this bitch in a crowd, I wouldn't be able to point her out.

Anyhow, according to my girlfriends, she would ask them in-depth questions about me and my stripping, to the point where she would creep them out. Well, she found out which club I worked at and started working there. At first, I was like this girl looks familiar... then my girlfriends filled me in on how she got a job at the same club as me. It wasn't until 3 shifts in that I put two and two together that this was the same girl. Strange, right? Wouldn't you introduce yourself and say 'hey, man... I live with your besties at RIC... my name is so and so."?? Nope! Not even a friendly smile or hello! The creep factor set in hard when she chose the name "Viviana" (so close to "Tatiana", no?) and was wearing her hair just like me!

By the second week, she had gotten similar costumes (like broke down, low rent versions of my costumes) like mine and was already trying to hustle MY clients while I was in the dressing room or on stage. It was BANANAS! So, after a few weeks, I had had it. I rallied up my best girls at the club to stake out the dressing room while I sprinkled ITCHING POWDER into her costume bag, specifically on her thongs. It was still early in the night, so I was prepared for shit to go down during peak business hours. There it was! She FINALLY went for a costume change! (PS. You know a dancer is lame when they wear the same costume for more than one set during the same night.) Ha! 'Viviana' goes on stage as an itching WRECK, while me and my cohorts were watching from afar in sheer satisfaction! She ran off stage and got management.

The head boss came down to the dressing room (you know it's serious when the boss rears his head in the dressing room) and asked what was going on. Being the solid bitch that I am, I said I don't know and that I had a client waiting for me upstairs. The boss excused me. Then, Viviana yells out that it was all my fault and that I had done something to her costumes. My boss was FURIOUS that a new girl would accuse one his best money makers of something ridiculous. So he screamed for Viviana to pack her shit and get the fuck out! Ha! And so, she did! Miserable and defeated, Viviana left with her small collection of broke down costumes and left. It wasn't even 9pm yet.

Later on, I would see her from afar on campus and had heard she went to another club and used my stage name 'Tatiana'. My girlfriends from the dorm ostracized her from all dorm activities and she was eventually transferred to another dormitory. And that was that! Crazy bitch!

CHAPTER 14
HEROINE OR HEROIN?

Being in a club environment, you were bound to run into a few drug addicts here or there or here AND there. There was one girl I will never forget…. a very tall, lanky, skeletal dancer with absolutely no tits whatsoever of Indian decent that went by the name of Sequoia. Her laughs and kindness were captivating at the beginning of the shift, so when it went deeper into the night and her methadone or heroin was wearing off, her laughs were replaced my seizures and shakes… also known as the withdrawals an addict experiences called 'the heroine shakes'.

Witnessing a person going through the 'shakes' is difficult knowing that NOTHING, except heroin or methadone, can help this person. It really sucked that this would happen to a pretty cool chick that I actually liked talking to. It was truly as if a demon had taken over her body and us girls were trying to perform an exorcism between stage shows and lap dances. And the management didn't know what to do, except, just let her 'shake' it off, I guess. This turned out to be a regular thing… 'oh someone cover Sequoia's stage set; she's got the shakes.' It got to the point where she was asked not to come back to the club until she cleaned up her act, which was on and off for a few years. The last time I saw Sequoia, she was still using and was sleeping in the corner of the dressing room with the needle still in her toes. I still wonder about whatever happened to Sequoia from time to time.

CHAPTER 15
RIDE AND ALMOST DIE

Speaking of drug addicts, it was early in my career and I was still sweet and polite to everyone I met at the club. The bitch switch hadn't kicked in yet. This new girl and I became fast friends and decided to dance a set together.

She was pretty subdued, which I found out later that she was on some kind of downer the whole night. She liked one of my costumes, so I let her borrow it. It was a lace zipper dress with a rubber lining. It wasn't that special, but it was a damn hot dress. Well, NEVER lend anything to anyone in that business, because you will never see that shit again! It was the end of the night and she was telling me this long-winded story about how her boyfriend was supposed to pick her up that night, but bailed and that she has a 3-year-old girl waiting at home for her. At this point, I had made way more money than her that night but didn't think that maybe it's a ploy to jump. She asked me if she would giver her a ride into South Providence and drop her off at home. It was 2am. I felt bad, so I said yes. She was still wearing my dress. I asked for it back and she replied that she wanted to wash it for me, and she'd give it back to me at our next shift. Gullible me, I said ok.

So, we get in my car and drive about 15 minutes to the heart of the ghetto at 2:30am. At this point, the girl had almost fallen asleep from whatever drugs she was on. I still needed her to tell me her address! So, I blast the music hoping she would wake, which she did and just got out of the car on a random street corner and started walking aimlessly.... There were lots of unsavory thugs and whatnots out and about watching and they all started to approach my car. As soon as she shut the car door, I locked the doors, and I floored it to the next highway entrance! I never saw the girl again or that hot dress again! I also learned my lesson.... Never lend or do favors for a drug addict, no matter how bad you feel for them. Life is full of choices and the choices we make, we have to live with.

CHAPTER 16
MOTHER ANGELA

Very rarely do you run into good people in the sleazy, nightclub business. One of these good people was an older cougar named Angela. Angela was a 40 something very fit, slender tan beautiful mature woman with a fabulous set of silicone tits. If I remember correctly, they were 450cc silicone boobs on a 110 lb. frame, which translates to nice gigantic boobs, but not side show freak boobs. She also was the mother of five children and married to a fireman! Her stomach was perfect. Any who, she had so much wisdom and wit and was very open-minded about sex.

One day, I was feeling all crappy about myself about all the bitches shit talking me at the club and she came over and cheered me up with all kinds of stories and wisdom about 'how it's lonely at the top' and 'you must be doing something right if you're the center of gossip'. Over the years, she had become a good friend and mentor. I admired her no-nonsense approach to the business. We just reconnected recently through Facebook and am happy to find she's doing well!

CHAPTER 17
CHARLOTTE THE HARLOT

They say imitation is the best form of flattery. Whoever said that quote is frigging' moron that never experienced imitation to begin with! When someone has an original look and you're not a famous person, it just becomes a brawl of who did it first and who did it better. At least if a famous person gets imitated, then it can qualify as flattery because everyone has seen the original already. But if someone who is not well-known yet gets ripped off, too bad for that someone with the original idea. There's no way to really prove it you were the original, unless you have witnesses or photographic evidence. And back in the late 90's, there were no smart phones and social media, yet... so good luck with documentation!

At my college there was yet another creepy girl that would watch what I would do and wear.... except, unlike Itching Powder Viviana, she was in our circle of acquaintances and friends. Her name was Charlotte. She was a thin, white girl with long wavy dark hair parted in the middle and black-lined raccoon eyes that listened to way too much Tori Amos and mentioned she was a sexually molested survivor to anyone that would listen, including people she had just met a few minutes prior. I'm sorry it happened, if it happened, but she was really just using it as a ploy for attention. Super annoying and not fair to others who have gone through a similar traumatic experience. I quickly gave her the moniker of 'Charlotte the Harlot' after she would date all my ex-boyfriends after we would break up. It was a strange habit of hers.

Slowly, she began to wear similar clothes as me and all of sudden be into the same things I was into, like techno music and raves and DJ-ing. I had my own radio show for four years on college radio WXIN 99.7 Ground Zero Radio in Providence. Stoners would listen to my show since I was on around 4pm... which I always thought it was perfect for high tea. Apparently, I was on right during 4:20, so the request line would always blow up with stoners around 4:20 -ish requesting shit like Rusted Root and Dave Matthews Band, to which I would just play more German happy hardcore, just to fuck with their baked brains...hahaha. Although she tried to DJ, she lost interest after a week and went back to be a boring ass beeotch.

After dating ex number two, she decided to get in on the exotic dancing business, but didn't want to be 'touched'. Now, Rhode Island has a semi-contact law in strip clubs. Guys were able to touch the dancer only on the sides. No touching on the butt, boobs or inside the legs and contact lap dances were allowed. I thought this law was pretty fair and the dancer also had the upper hand on whether they were ok with that or not. Just 20 minutes over the border to Connecticut and Massachusetts (also Vermont and New Hampshire) (on the flip side ,Upstate New York had a full contact law: able to touch ANYWHERE on the dancer (I wasn't down for that, FYI), the strip club laws differed in the way that there was absolutely no contact. A plexiglass would separate the dancers from the clients. Now, if I were a dude, I would totally drive an extra 20-25 minutes to Rhode Island to get a better 'experience' for my money. A bigger bang for the buck, if you will. Because of these law disparities, girls in Rhode Island would make easy 5- 10 times more money per night than a dancer in Connecticut or

Massachusetts. Hence, the influx of all sorts of dancers invading the Rhode Island strip clubs. This was also a reason why I did not really budge from the club I worked at. While other transient dancers were working my club, I had already nabbed the cream of the crop clients, that might I add, drove in from other states. I was set.

Back to Charlotte the Harlot... she had decided to give exotic dancing a go after seeing the riches the job brought me. So, I gave her a pro-tip because I'm so damn nice, that maybe Connecticut or Massachusetts would fit her needs better. Within a few days, I heard she was dancing at a club in New Haven, Connecticut. Now, New Haven is known to be meth central of Southern New England. In Northern New England, Lowell, Massachusetts takes that cake. So, I can only imagine the quality of clientele that club would attract. I heard through the grapevine that she, too, took my dancing name 'Tatiana' (can't they come up with another slutty name... really?) and was trying to make burlesque happen in New Haven with budget versions of my costumes.

So, after a few months, I had heard she was trying to make it sound like I was copying her... a true SINGLE WHITE FEMALE! Side note: A great film to scare the shit out of you from getting any roommates.

In our circle of friends, she started spreading rumors on how I shit talked behind my friends' backs. I lost a few friends because of her lies. Whatever, she was dancing in the most destitute club in New England- HA!

The following semester I didn't see her on campus at all. Rumor had it that she dropped out of college and was a full-time, day shift, exotic dancer in Connecticut. Okay, day shifts were usually reserved for single mothers with c-section scars and full-time drug addicts. Not that there's anything wrong with that... I had a c-section with my third child, but I had quit dancing a decade before. What I mean is, the hotness quality of dancers plummets during the day shifts... the real hot, professional strippers are booked during prime times like Friday/Saturday nights. What I'm trying to get at is that Charlotte the Harlot ended up being in a shitty place... even after trying to run me through the mud. Karma is a bitch!

CHAPTER 18
HOT DRUNK TWINS

Working in a strip club for many years affords you to meet all sorts of girls from all walks of life. I mean, one minute you're changing next to a Pre-med student from Brown University and then the next minute you're standing next to a crack whore from South Providence with two baby daddies and exactly 14 teeth left in her mouth. It's a wide range, I'd say. Then there were the house girls... the girls who were not transient dancers looking to make a quick buck. House girls are 'career' exotic dancers, which I was. We would keep an eye on the club and make sure the transient girls play by the rules, so the quality of customers didn't dip and furthermore, the quantity of cash would flow well throughout the club. Because, say, a transient girl is offering hand jobs in the back for the price of a lap dance... that would just cut into the other girls' business... and bring in sleazy, cheap clients.

The house girls wanted to keep the high rollers coming in, but also keep their attention with the transient girls, as long as they played by the rules. It all became a game of snitching and she said/she said and just a catty mess overall. So, the house girls would stick together and monitor the transient girls and the transient girls would have no choice, but to watch their backs. That's why when you're the new girl in a club, you have to be as low key and meek as possible. Because you never know who is going to support you or go against you in the beginning. It could literally cost you your job. So, as a house girl, I had a network of ladies and we all would stick together and have each other's backs.

There were these two house girls, Nadine and Justine, that were not sisters in real life, but looked like sisters and always were a team on stage. I'm not going to lie.... They were hot as fuck. Both were tan, skinny blondes with long hair and had natural C-cup, ski slope tits. They were the ultimate bimbo fantasy for any hot-blooded, white trash male. Their shows included a football jersey cut right at the bottom of the nipple, just enough to show the very sexy, under-boob and the thigh high leather boots accompanied by the most severe 1980's hair band music you could possibly think of. They nailed that sector quite brilliantly and I admired that, especially, since a) they would never cut into my clientele and b) since we had such contrasting looks. I think they viewed me as the stuck up, gothic, lingerie bitch, but we all acknowledged each other with the house girl camaraderie.

Nadine and Justine loved to party and drinking on the job was just business as usual. Let me tell you, drinking on the job, any job, is probably not a good choice. Money gets lost, clients take advantage of shortchanging you, and your reflexes for bringing in clients to the private dance area is pretty dodgy and slow. Not to mention, being late to the stage is an ultimate no-no in the business and well, Nadine and Justine didn't really give a fuck about that. You would think they would get fired because of their antics, but one was actually the boss's son's girlfriend and the other was fucking the DJ, so they were pretty solid job-wise.

I mention them because I found them to be brilliant in the way that they operated their business, even though it probably wasn't intentional. They would leave the audience wanting more by being late and unpredictable. They had nailed the aesthetics by copying 1980s hair band sluts, like in Van Halen and Whitesnake music videos. They had capitalized on local football team hysteria that seems to captivate their carefully curated clients. They had set themselves apart by teaming up together and pretending to be sisters. And lastly, they were having fun even though they could probably make more if they wanted to by curbing the drinking. So, was this all by accident? Probably. But in my book, it was the most genius thing I had ever seen in a titty bar. So, hats off, or shall I say, tops off to a spectacular duo, Justine and Nadine!

CHAPTER 19
PATRIOTS MILF

If you have ever been to New England, you probably are familiar with the insanity aligned to the New England Patriots. That football team are like living gods around these parts. The famed football team (before Tom Brady) were a constant fixture at the club. They would take up probably half the club and spend virtually no money. They figured they were footballers and probably could get dances and more for free, which would make me ponder why they would go to a strip club in the first place? I used to stay away from them, because a) They were cheap and b) They were cocky and c) I was too goth and weird for them.

Anyway, one of the dancers that used to lure them to our club was a former Patriots cheerleader named Paige. Paige was what you call today a MILF. She was a 40 plus woman, a bit on the muscular, mannish side, but pretty decent looking. She had shoulder length, dirty blonde hair and could easily pass for a bank teller during the day. Because of her former cheerleading connections, she had virtually fucked every single team member and loved to tell us girls in the dressing room stories about her conquests. Her stories were captivating, yet obviously embellished. No one, not even Hugh Hefner, could have wild times like that every single night... or could they? Nonetheless, her adventures were highly entertaining and very empowering for any woman at the time and pretty trail-blazing for a woman her age at that time. I remember I used to want to be half as experienced as her when I get at her age. So, tops off to Paige and her bewildering stories about the New

England Patriots! I'll never look at the New England Patriots the same way again!

CHAPTER 20
SATIVA GOES ON A TRIP

There was this really stunning raver chick that I had befriended at the club...her stage name was Sativa (named after a type of Weed). She was in her late teens with shoulder-length honey blonde hair, tan, athletic build with newly fake tits that looked more like Tupperware ... probably because they were too new and hadn't dropped or softened, yet. In any case, she was gorgeous and a cool chick. We had hung out several times outside the club and I quickly found she was a fan of ecstasy and special K. While I loved to go to raves, I identified as 'straight-edge' and stayed away from drugs. My recreational druggie friends were cool with that and I always ended up being the designated driver.

One day she came into the club and said she had an amazing opportunity to go to Japan and become a model and possibly be in a Japan-based pop group. I was like... 'go for it, girl!'... and take me with you! The take me with you part never happened, but by the following week, Sativa had given her notice at the club and was on a plane to Japan. This was before social media and smart phones, so they were no snap chat stories of the journey or anything like that. So, when someone went on a trip, you'd have wait until their ass got back to show photos and tell you about the trip.

About six months later, Sativa walked into the club looking completely unrecognizable! She had lost her hotness... her hair was a choppy, secretarial 'may I speak to the manager' length... she had gained weight and had a look of despair and sadness in her eyes. She was shell of what she had been. Speaking to her was not the fun-loving Sativa I knew six months prior. We all gathered around and asked about her experience in Japan... unfortunately, she never made it to Japan. She was tricked into falling into a sex slave ring in Bangkok. Somehow, she escaped and made it back to the US, but not unscathed. We all had so many questions that she wasn't ready to answer. Sativa worked at the club for no more than a month more, when she quit and disappeared. Clearly, drugs and despair had gotten the best of her. I wonder where Sativa is these days, but really, I think my beautiful friend had truly disappeared the day she had left for 'Japan'.

CHAPTER 21
ATM STAKE-OUT

My favorite spot to hangout at the club was the ATM. It was perfect. Near the front door so you could see who was coming in and out, and able to see who took out how much from the ATM. It was also conveniently positioned close to the Private Dance area. It was a brilliant strategic position and every girl knew that was my 'spot'. Men are very simple creatures, so if you're in the right place at the right time, it could mean the difference between an okay night and a good night. So, I had a lot of 'stray' (stray meaning not regular clients) clients that might have been on a time constraint (on lunch break or whatever) and just wanted a private dance without all the chit chat bullshit.

That's where I came in... situated by the ATM right near the private dance area, while the other girls were sitting down in a far corner of the club getting drunk and gossiping, most likely about me. My strategy was getting the 'strays', but more importantly, get the quality, long-term clients for a high return. I would try and turn the 'strays' into long-term clients. Some would fall for it, some wouldn't, but in the end, I made out fantastically cash-wise. Always be near an ATM.

CHAPTER 22
BOUNCERS

There were so many odd characters at the club and I'm mostly talking about the people who worked there. The crew of bouncers were a pretty funny bunch. Most of them had the dress code of shaved heads and meathead expressions all wrapped up in tuxedo shirts and bowties. Each one looked like they could snap a guy in half AND snap into a Slim Jim.

I had a good repertoire with the bouncers because they were pretty much my personal bodyguards. Any problems I had with clients, which were rare and far between, they could resolve it with just a look. The head bouncer, Gabe, would walk me to my car personally every night after my shift. I would tip him extra to do so, because I was exiting the club with the most cash most nights and didn't want to get jumped by a group of crackhead strippers (not all of the them were crackheads). Gabe was a funny bastard. He would make all kinds of lewd jokes and be pretty candid about stripper issues, like "Are you on your period? Because you're an 8 today, when usually you're a 10." Snide, yet hilarious remarks like that. Some girls took it badly, but I took it as a great opportunity for snide banter. For years, Gabe was my personal bodyguard in the club and my go- to for any problems, including personal issues, like boyfriend problems. Later on, I found out that he had been stealing from the management at the club. I've lost touch with him since I exited the business, but if I ever become a world-famous actress in need of a bodyguard, I know who to call!

CHAPTER 23

SAUDI EXPORTS

Working in the club, you meet a lot of different people. A handful of 'nomadic' career strippers would pass through around the holiday season. These 'nomadic career strippers' were mostly older women in their late thirties and early forties and still had banging bodies from tons of plastic surgery. They were the type of strippers that would do porn on the side. These were the ladies that didn't want the pressure of being a 'feature dancer'. Apparently, being a feature dancer required some type of planning for their tour, where these 'career strippers' were more of a nomadic variety… leaving the club at their own whim if the money dried up for them.

The internet was still blossoming, so some of these ladies were the first internet porn stars. They hailed from everywhere from Florida, New York, New Jersey and even California. They would just pass through the club as they traveled around the country in packs of three or four. These 'nomadic career strippers' knew the game well and played their hands efficiently. They knew when to keep going or when to quit and move on to the next club. I would befriend these nomads, more because a) they made the club nicer and more professional and b) they were all business and were focused on money just like me c) most of them didn't do drugs or even drink, so they were interesting to talk to, a wealth of knowledge, if you will.

One slow night, I overheard the pack say they are moving to another club the next night and were complaining about how the business was waning for them, even with the constant travel and new clients. So, I decided to join in and wish them a warm farewell. We started chatting and one of the girls mentioned that she may be taking off for Saudi Arabia at the end of the month. She said her agency had given her an offer by a Saudi Royal to join his 'harem' again. She was a typical gorgeous, porn star looking woman with bleach blonde hair, tanned skin and huge 32EE fake tits (which in my opinion were a bit wonky, but her beautiful face made up for it). She was the 'classiest' looking out of the bunch regarding her costumes. My ears perked up when she said 'Saudi Royal.' Everyone knows the Saudis shit bricks of gold and can be some of the most generous people on earth. Hell, even the Clintons were in bed with them! So, we all leaned in and had so many questions for her... how much will they pay, what is expected from her, will they make her wear a veil?

Apparently, she had been invited the previous year and had stayed for a total of three months at the Saudi Royal Palace. She couldn't say exactly which Prince or royal she was exclusive to because 'they all looked alike and had the same last name'. Ok, I totally understand that. She said she was given her own suite, but was given a schedule of events to prep for. Basically, she would join them for dinner at 11pm and spend the night and early morning dancing and 'entertaining' the guests and royals. I asked her straight up, 'Do you have to have sex? Or is it just 'dancing'? ... bless her heart, she was so candid... she had to have sex with not only the royals, but with any guest that the royals wanted to 'entertain'. It was part of her 'contract'.

Okay, that was pretty obvious, but I needed to know the nitty gritty of it all... after all, maybe I could sign up?? This sounded like an adventure! The busty dancer continued with her wild story of how they kept tigers as pets unleashed and that essentially everyone over there is like a vampire – sleep all day/up all night because of the extreme heat. And that they are not religious when it comes to sex... it's all a show for the people of Saudi Arabia. She said the palace has orgies virtually every night with high-profile guests and wealthy royals. Also, that the 'harem' is made up of entirely blonde haired, blue-eyed Playboy models and porn stars from every corner of America shipped in from an agency in Miami. This was all very fascinating to me! So how much was the pay? Where there any restrictions??

    She continued with her big blue eyes and said the pay was 'very generous'... enough for her to buy two houses and put her kid through college. They wire the money to her bank account, before she even arrives to prepay any of her bills for the three-month trip. Then, upon arrival, she gets her own suite with a butler, is given a blood test and gynecological exam and is given gifts daily that include, designer dresses, handbags and jewelry. At one point, a guest had given her a Bentley, but was unable to take it with her back to the States for some reason.

    Ironically, the 'harem' was never to leave the Royal compound unchaperoned and even had to be chaperoned around the grounds as not to run into the many wives and children of the men. Also, the 'harem' was allowed to go out once a month to a mall chaperoned with a driver and bodyguard to go on a shopping spree. It all sounded very Playboy Mansion to me, but with a terrifying consequence. She also filled us in on the abundance of drugs, mostly hashish. She also mentioned the plight of a girl that they 'grew tired' of and kicked her out before her contract was over and made her pay her own airfare back.

As for Busty Dancer, they liked her so much, that they invited her back again for another three months. So, as the club was winding down, I couldn't help myself into asking for the contact of the agency in Miami. She looks me right in the eye and says, 'Oh, they'll never hire you…. You have dark hair and natural tits and I can tell you're feisty. The Saudis don't like that.' Well, that was that. I'd probably complain about the food, anyway. I like to look at it as a blessing in disguise. My whole life trajectory would've been completely different, and I would be a different person seeing that being a prostitute could be damaging to the psyche for some. Also, leaving my cats for three months would've been the deal-breaker. Every time I see the Saudi Royal Family on the news, I can't help to think if my porn star friend had 'entertained' them the night before.

CHAPTER 24

99 Problems… and the Liquor License was one of them

The club I was working at as a house girl was going through some legal battles with the city regarding ordinance- revoking the liquor license, etc… it was really the residents of the town that didn't want that kind of establishment in their neighborhood. We were actually a very clean and orderly club compared to the shit holes in Providence.

So, for about a few months, we had to not be topless or nude anymore, but liquor was still served. Our house mother had a brilliant idea of using liquid latex to cover our nipples and the width of our nipple going under our breasts. It was genius. I knew exactly where to get the liquid latex! I had modeled for a store in Providence called Miko's and the owner and I were pretty tight. I had called him up one day and asked him to order me NUDE color liquid latex. A week later, I got a call and picked it up. I also had informed him to stock up on BLACK liquid latex because of the situation our club was going through. Bam! Every girl at the club had black dots in their tits … it looked really unattractive and the club patrons were visibly displeased. But, I went on stage with NUDE sprinkled with glitter latex nipple covers… it looked like had nothing on! The cops couldn't get me! HA! Girls were oohing and ahhhhing about how natural it looked… I was booking lap dances left and right as if nothing had happened!

Soon girls wanted the nude liquid latex, except my buddy at Miko's said they only offered black latex, honoring my request. Ha! My plan worked! By the way, this was before Internet shopping and Amazon, so if a store didn't have an item, well, you were screwed. You'd have to wait weeks, sometimes months for things to arrive.

    A few months of this ridiculousness passed by and the club owners were ready to set up shop in another state- Tennessee to be exact. They had bought a CHURCH and turned it into a strip club called 'CONFESSIONS'. I have to say that was a pretty brilliant idea. They wanted to fly me and 3 other girls down to Tennessee to open the club. I was all for it, except I had a trip to Cannes planned with Troma. So, I declined. Shortly after that, they closed the club in Rhode Island and spent their full attention at the club in Tennessee. I never saw my boss and his wife until years later after I had quit the business.

CHAPTER 25

THE FOXY LADY

It was late May of 2000 when I came back from the French Riviera ready to move on to a new club. I already knew I was Foxy Lady material. The Foxy Lady was known at the time to be one of the upscale clubs in Providence and in Brockton, Mass. The one in New Bedford was the crack central one where management would send you if you were in trouble or had been pink slipped for gaining weight, chipped nail polish, etc.

Anyway, I went in on a Monday for amateur night won the grand prize of $500 and by Tuesday night, I was starting my first shift. I had contacted all my clients to see me at the Foxy. The Foxy was more of a corporate atmosphere. There were a lot more bullshit payouts and tons of t-shirt selling. We had to sell a t-shirt every god damn hour. If we didn't, we would have to buy the shirt. It was really set up to keep the dancer poor and busy on stupid stuff that only benefited the club. Therefore, the turnover was high. I managed to maneuver through all the BS and actually, scored a coveted locker of my own. I didn't need to haul a huge suitcase anymore. I would just arrive, sit in the makeup chair, get my hair and makeup done professionally and slide on stage with not a minute to spare. It was way more glamorous than the previous club, but boy, did you pay for it.

The Foxy even had an oil wresting ring downstairs that was in full force on the weekends. There also was a full women's locker room with showers and a Jacuzzi, and a masseuse just for the dancers round the clock. But, we also had the pressure of making an insane amount of money to just keep up. I remember leaving the club a few nights with a negative amount of money from when I walked in. This means I would come in, work for 6 -8 hours and leave PAYING the management $50. It was humiliating to put on shows all night and have to give all your tips plus $50 to the house. So, I scaled back my hours to work only when my clients would come in.

One night, I was having an awful night. Tim came in to see me and I began to cry. We were in the champagne room and I explained to him how tired I was of dancing. At this point, the Bed & Breakfast (a house I bought on foreclosure and renovated with my mother into a B & B) was just barely breaking even (it was after 9/11, so tourism was down), but I still had a bank loan that needed to be paid off to generate an income. I asked Tim if he could pay that loan off... it was only $30,000 and I would quit dancing if I could just pay that off. He agreed. The next morning, I got an exact amount from the bank and had Tim write a check for that amount.

The following week I gave my notice at the club and invited all of my clients all week to celebrate my retirement. I remember my last night vividly. I had cleaned out my locker; I had a fantastic dinner at the club with my clients and had a special stage show before my official send off into the 'real' world. At this point, I had only kept two clients to see after retirement- Tim and Jack. We would still do lunch and go shopping. My relationship with my clients had really evolved into friendships at this point.

I had officially retired from stripping in January of 2002 at the age of 25, clocking in at nearly eight years as an exotic dancer. After Tim paid off my mortgage, I thought it would be a good idea to have him finance a film starring me. I mean, what a better way to break into Hollywood, right? So, we planned a trip to Los Angeles to meet a French film producer/director, Emmanuel, that I had met at Sundance a few months prior. He would later become my husband.

CHAPTER 26
PLAYBOY

When I was little, I used to notice the special magazines behind the cash register... you know, the ones that had a half-hidden magazine cover... with only the magazine title and beautiful, pouty face popping out. Well, I was smart enough to know that there was something MAGICAL inside that magazine. Something that i wasn't supposed to see for some strange reason that couldn't understand at the time. My goal was to get my hands on one of those PLAYBOY magazines and see what the fuss is all about! And so, I did…. At age 13. Such gorgeous women! They're like Vogue models, but NAKED! Will I have boobs like that one day? If I pray to the Boobie Gods every night, maybe I will! …. "Are you there Boobie God? It's Me, Roxy." – by BOOBY Blume. From then on, I knew I wanted to be sexy, beautiful and confident like the ladies in the nudie magazine… and it had nothing to do with how boys would want me… I just thought they were so captivatingly gorgeous- period. I had decided at age 13 that this was the woman I wanted my future self to be.

It was my first year in college – the fall of 1995- I was 17, a few weeks shy of 18, (December baby) when I decided to enter my photo to Playboy. I had seen an ad for The College Edition of Playboy, which seemed to me to be the best chance of getting in. This was back before we had digital cameras in our phones with filters at your fingertips… it was the age of the DISPOSABLE CAMERAS. A disposable camera does not allow you to see the image until after you have it developed at a One-

Hour Photo Mat. Not only that, you only had like 24 shots, so you only had 24 chances to get a decent shot.

So, I had my disposable camera ready and went over a girlfriend's place to get that lucky shot. I quickly realized my girlfriend's apartment had shitty lighting. Whatever, we'll call it 'mood' lighting. Also, my girlfriend was a hardcore PHISH fan… so there were a lot of tie dye and concert posters on the walls. WTF am I to do?? The shower and kitchen areas were out because they were super dirty and well, poising on toilet or sink is probably not that sexy in most circles. I reluctantly got naked and decided to take photos on her bed with a tie-dye bedspread. Whatever, thankfully, it was definitely a college themed… a grunge-y, stoner sorority lair, if you will.

The next morning, I took the camera to be developed at a One-Hour photo mat. These ancient relics were a tiny building usually in the middle of a desolate parking lot where you would drop off your camera/film to be developed with the hour. It was a little embarrassing knowing that the middle-aged man behind the counter was going to see your treasure trove of photos while developing them. It was an unavoidable awkwardness, to say the least. An hour passed by and I sheepishly paid and took my photos and ran to my car. The excitement! The suspense! Did I close my eyes in half the shots? Did I remember to 'elongate' my neck? Did I cheat my body to the side for a slimmer look? It would all come down to it momentarily…. I feverishly looked through the stack of 24 photos to see if one came out decent. Yes! One ….and one only would make it as an entry to Playboy. Although, the background was cringe-y, I looked –dare I say…good?! I had that over highlighted Carmen Electra hair, the thin waif eyebrows and porcelain skin. Maybe a bit too gothic, but who cares – I was sending it to Playboy! And off it went with a lick of a stamp via snail mail....

A few weeks later, Playboy contacted me and wanted to use the photo in their 1996 College Edition... I was so excited, except I soon realized that they would use my real name and college. I was so terrified of being found out by my family, especially since I had just started exotic dancing a few months prior without their knowledge. I had just turned 18 and was quite timid and shy and put too much weight on what people would think. This was a time when posing nude would keep you from getting a 'real' job in the future. Just look at what Vanessa Williams had to go through... she had to give up her Miss America crown because she posed nude for Playboy at one time! Crazy, right?! Anyway, I turned it down and that moment and decision was the biggest regret of my life to this day.

A few years later in 1999, I decided to give Playboy another shot. I was more mature and less 'green' about certain things. Also, I was at the peak of my career as an exotic dancer and fetish model. I looked the part, I acted the part ... hell, I was the part! So, I got a call for an audition as a host for a late-night show on the Playboy Channel. I made it through two rounds of auditions at the now-closed Playboy Enterprises on Fifth Avenue between 57th and 56th street in NYC. The competition was stiff... no pun ... yes pun. So many gorgeous girls that looked pretty identical... big tits, skinny body and long blonde hair. In the end, I lost out, but it was my 2nd chance at being part of Playboy again. At least I gave it another shot, even though I failed. I guess it wasn't meant to be, after all.

PART TWO

PART TWO

THIS IS ACTING?

Growing up and living in Rhode Island was really great. It was only a 45-minute train ride to Boston and a 3-hour bus, or train ride to NYC. It was the best of both worlds... small town feel, but less than an hour away from the big city. Sometimes, I would drive to NYC in less than 2 hours and 15 minutes in my little, vamp-colored 1985 328 BMW... that was without traffic. But I would opt for the bus usually because a) I didn't have to park my car in a garage in the city and b) I could sleep, study or prep my lines.

Sometimes, I would miss the Greyhound, Peter Pan or Bonanza Bus back home to Rhode Island, so I would sleep in the Port Authority with mace in one hand and my flip phone in the other, while dressed in fur and whatnot. (A flip phone was an ancient relic of the 1990s. You could only receive and send out calls and texts in an analog way, which was the precursor to emojis- for instance 143 meant 'I Love You' or 8008 spelled 'BOOB'- primitive, right? anyhow, I only know one adult and 2 teens who still have a flip phone today- they shall remain nameless.) I did that often enough to start recognizing the bums. This was before Disney bought 42nd street and revitalized into basically a Mid-western strip mall with a Dave & Buster's and Starbucks, among other mundane establishments. That whole area was a very seedy part of the city. Lots of titty bars, 25 cent peep shows and dive bars, none of which I had ever worked at. Later on, I would work at Scores in midtown for a short period (more on that later) and other clubs in other cities.

On more than one occasion, if I missed the last 9:30 bus, I would go downtown and spend the evening until the morning hours at gay nightclubs, like SPA or Limelight. One cold blustery evening I had a fur coat on, the beautiful transvestite at the door wouldn't let me in because I was wearing fur. This fur coat was the only really warm jacket I had that could withstand the frosty, windy weather. Also, I had bought it at a very deep, discount at the local Salvation Army in North Providence, RI. I like to think it belonged to a slain mafia wife for dramatic soap opera sake. Any who, this fur coat was very important to me. So, I went to the alley around the corner and put my coat inside out and hid it behind a dumpster praying some crackhead wouldn't find it and well, smoke it up. I went back to the nightclub and the transvestite let me in. I stayed until 4 am watching a bunch of people tweak their asses off to happy hardcore music. Then I took the 5am bus home, getting home just in time to shower, eat and go to a 9 am English Lit class at Rhode Island College and then later to work at the strip club. I'm not saying I would fall asleep in class, but I did have the occasional spiral notebook mark on my face.

CHAPTER 1
SUBURBAN BARBIE

One day, I got a call to dress as Barbie at a Westchester, NY Toys R' Us. I took the job because a) I love Barbie and b)I was being paid CASH MONAY. Also, I was the only petite, size 2 model available that day from the agency. Any who, I show up at the store that is just outside of NYC... Westchester is the wealthy suburbs of NYC... mostly families with parents working in the city, since it's only a 30 minute train ride into the city.

I show up and the hum-drum cashier with fake long, hot pink nails directs me to the employee backroom. It smelled of potatoes and nail polish. That lady is definitely painting her nails on break and eating baked potatoes for lunch, I presumed. She hands me a busted, blonde, polyester wig out of a plastic bag and a wrinkled Barbie Princess dress that fit me perfectly. A few minutes later, I transformed into a busted Barbie from the 'burbs and was ready to greet the children. Ah, yes... the children.... At the time I was not yet married and had no children. As a matter of fact, I had ZERO experience with kids. I peeked out of the backroom and saw a line of sweet young girls waiting patiently in line to meet, 'Barbie'. Some were crying, some were whining, and some were screaming in excitement. I was trapped and I wanted to get it over with like tearing off a bandage. I made my grand entrance with little girls pulling at my dress vying for my attention. Trapped? No... more like AMBUSHED! The parents seemed leerier of me than the kids. These kids ACTUALLY thought I was Barbie!

After snapping what seemed to be a billion photos, smiling through my gritted teeth, and bullshitting little girls with Barbie-isms, my shift had ended. In some ways, it was cool, and, in some ways, I just wanted to rip my wig off and say, 'Calm the fuck down, ladies!'. In any case, I wish I had photographic evidence of the event, but the cashier with the long, fake pink nails took a photo with her disposable camera and was supposed to snail mail a photo to me after she got the camera developed. See? Aren't we glad for smart phones?! I never received the photo after all... I guess she was too busy painting her long ass nails and eating potatoes in the break room. Whatever, I got to be Barbie for the day- any girl's dream!

CHAPTER 2
MTV

Back in the day, MTV had a little show called 'Total Request Live" ... it was shot at the Viacom studio in Times Square with a huge window the size of a city block. As you were walking on the street in the afternoon (somewhere from 3pm-5pm to be exact), you could see the show unfold before your very eyes a few floors up. It was hosted by Carson Daly and featured all the hottest acts of the time- Britney Spears, Eminem, Salt N' Pepa, Green Day- you name it! What was so exciting about this particular show, was that a) it was live – so anything these unpredictable rock stars would do would get caught on the show b)there was tremendous audience participation- in the street or in the studio c)this was a time before social media or internet really, so this was kind of like a social event- like 'hey man, did you see what Christina Aguilera wore on TRL today?' – it was like a live fashion/music magazine! TRL was like watching the cool kid's table at the high school cafeteria. You took notes.

I was always mesmerized by anything MTV. My dream was to become a host of an MTV program or something.... That and also to become a Fly Girl on 'In Living Color'. The Fly girl never panned out, BUT the MTV thing worked out twice in my life.

Once, I amazingly booked an MTV commercial! I was super duper excited! I got all the details from agency- I was ready! I arrived bright and early for my call time at the famed Silvercup Studios. So early that I was able to meander inside the different sound stages and see everything from a 1970s subway car interior to a Martian planet set. My young eyes were fixated! But duty called and I arrived on set for the MTV commercial after a quick look-y loo.

The shoot was simple and underwhelming. They told me to wear something you would wear at a rock concert- so leather mini-skirt, cropped, baby doll t-shirt and big black boots it was. I met the young, diminutive director who gave me very simple instructions. "You're a Groupie walking backstage after the show". Ummm, ok. That's easy. After, a few takes I was done. It was the fastest job I had ever done. They didn't even have me meet the 'band' or anything. Apparently, the 'band was a fictional OASIS type of rock band. I was sort of bummed not to have scenes with them, but whatever, I would make it in time for an earlier bus back home. So, I shot my very short MTV commercial scene, got paid $100 and only saw the commercial air maybe 4 times in a period of one month. And on top of that- they only showed me from the back walking down a very long hall. I didn't care- I was on MTV, at long last!

My other brush with MTV was when they held a NYC-wide search for MTV's next Veejay. This was after they had found the gem known as Jesse Camp. So, I guess the execs thought finding another Veejay off the street would be perfect for MTV. This would prove to be chaotic, but a fun challenge. After coaxing by a few friends to go for it, I was in…. it would require an overnight stay on the streets of NYC and lots of balls. The balls I had, but staying awake in line for 18 hours… not sure. I had only had a couple of days to figure things out, like what to wear and say before the Veejay audition. Finally, I found my perfect outfit! A Jean – Paul Gaultier Ganesh dress with an orange faux fur shrug. My hair? Shirley temple pig tails, of course, extra crunchy. I thought it was the perfect mix of punk, spirituality and supermodel in one- it was sort of like a spiritual Club Kid- James St. James would've approved! Anyway, I was set and ready to go! I had my little British Flag messenger bag with some food and more importantly, make up bag. I figured I would pull an all nighter, so no need for a blanket of anything. What I did forget was a warm jacket! I froze my tits off all night, but a sweet guy gave me his jacket while we waited in line all night. Sure, he was a competitor, but damn I was cold, and he was cute in a Ducky from 'Pretty in Pink ' kind of way! I got in line at 7pm the night before and made it to the audition room by 11am the next day.

    It was crazy, exhausting and insane, but I'm so glad I did it! I seized the day even though I failed! I met some really cool people along the way and had an unforgettable experience auditioning for MTV execs. No regrets!

CHAPTER 3
HARLEQUIN STUDIOS

Never audition at 'Harlequin Studios'! It was the cheapest audition space in the Theater district and for a good reason. Actually, I think they knocked down the building and built condos now. It was probably the most rank building ever, the rats in that building have a party among the asbestos and stale air. Rickety stairs made this location a hazard to your health. Stay away from the decades old penny candy machine in the lobby.

I once auditioned for a little known show called "The Sopranos" in that building. At the time, it was a new show. I was up for the part of 'Adriana', the snitch girlfriend of Christopher. I didn't take the audition that seriously, because it was at Harlequin Studios, so I went in wearing my usual, everyday clothes- which was basically rave wear... plus it was a super hot, humid day, so I went in with the most frizzed out hair and sweaty face. Nonetheless, I didn't get a callback. Looking back on it, I looked most definitely far from a mafia girlfriend, but more a tweaking club kid. That was turning point me... always dress in character for any and all auditions, no matter what because you never know.

CHAPTER 4
NICE BOX

Vivienne Westwood had a boutique in Soho back in the day. I would make sure I visit the boutique every time I'd go to the city. One day I saw a leopard print in hot pink and peach/ mock horsehair train case. Years later, Carrie Bradshaw from 'Sex & the City' would carry the luggage in the same print in the famous going to Paris episode. My instinct told me to buy it- and so I did. It was the first time I had spent so much money on one little thing. What a strange feeling buying a luxury item for yourself... a definite guilty pleasure. $2500 later and an afternoon filled with ass kissing by a beautiful Vietnamese salesperson named Tracy, I returned to the bus station to go home with the overpriced, yet over-the-top train case in hand. On my way, with a spring in my step and a pink leopard box in my hand still reeling in utter bliss, a bum summed it all up in one phrase, "Nice Box", followed by an evil laugh. I had to laugh with him because, you see, in the Northeast, "box' is slang for a woman's vagina. When I see my train case in my closet, I always think, "Nice Box' and then enjoy a brief chuckle inside. I bet Carrie Bradshaw would chuckle, too.

CHAPTER 5

WINONA'S BUTT DOUBLE

One day, I got a casting call to be Winona Ryder's butt double in the movie "Autumn in NY". It was for a love scene shot between Winona and Richard Gere. It was at a strange hour, like at 8pm in the Wall Street district. *Fun fact: Wall Street becomes a ghost town after 6pm.*

I went into a building undergoing renovation and arrived at the 16th floor only to see an entire crew of film and set workers. I was quickly ushered to another room with other 'butt doubles', I assumed. Then, we were asked to take off our bottoms, leaving our thong underwear and turn around forming a sort of line up – like at a police station. It was hilarious! All this pomp and circumstance for a butt that will be passed off as Winona Ryder's butt! Couldn't Winona just show her butt??? It's not that serious, girl! It was all just weird.

The director came in, Joan Chen, and looked at each of our butts and told us individually why we didn't get the butt double part. My reason was 'you're too aerobicized". What the hell does that mean? At least she didn't say I had a fat ass. I came to find out, they needed a sickly, scrawny bum because Winona's character had terminal cancer.

I was slightly 'butt-hurt' and one hour later, I was back on the street looking for a cab that was going back uptown. Unfortunately, for me, when Wall Street becomes a ghost town, cabs don't come around. And so, I walked my 'aerobicized' butt uptown until I found a cab. And I didn't get to see Richard Gere out of it all!

CHAPTER 6
THE ROCKETTES

I had always dreamed of becoming a showgirl of some sort... and so I had decided to go for it and audition for The Rockettes! Now, being a short girl is not conducive to being a Rockette. I admit, I lied on my application and said I was a perfect 5'8" Amazonian woman. I didn't really think about what I would do when they would call me in for an audition. And so, I got the phone call for cattle –call style audition. A cattle call style audition is when they call all the actors and actresses to one place AT THE SAME TIME. So, it's very overwhelming and stressful and to say the least, time consuming.

I stood in line for a good three hours before I was seen. After three hours of waiting with giant girls in line, it was my turn... except as soon as the casting directors saw me, they said 'You're too short! Go home!" They didn't even question why I wrote 5'8" ... probably because they didn't really read my application... which was actually a good thing because how would I explain I shrank 6 inches in 5 days. Hmmm.... Another question for another day, I guess. The point is I tried and tried, and it didn't work out... which brings me to this....

Back in my day, if you didn't fit a certain physical criteria, you would be discarded. Today, there are so many opportunities for overweight, people with acne, etc... I guess you would call it 'body positive' today. What I don't see in that movement are body positivity for petite women! We are still trying to get noticed and be given opportunities that other 'flawed' women have. I put 'flawed' in quotes because I don't see being petite as a flaw... and that is one thing I'd like the modeling world to change... we're not overweight, we don't have a hideous skin condition, we're just fun-sized! Anyway, I hope I don't offend anyone, but I hope people include us petite ladies in your next social movement. We thank you in advance.

CHAPTER 7
BRATZ DOLL

Every year, NYC has a Toy Fair that brings all the major toymakers from across the world in one place for buyers to see the new product line. That includes new doll unveilings, new gadgets, and toys. I had gotten a call from an agency representing a new line called 'Bratz Dolls'. The company was still tweaking the way their dolls looked like before unveiling prototypes for the Toy Fair. Back then, the only real doll was Barbie... so 'Bratz Dolls' would be the only solid competition for Barbie.

I met with one of the doll designers at the agency- they were looking for a model to dress as a life-sized Bratz Doll. I remember they took a million Polaroids of me at every damn angle and then measured me with a measuring tape for a good hour. At the time and I still do, I had a beauty mark under my left eye that I had drawn on and later tattooed permanently since the age of 14. I had been inspired by Sherilyn Fenn from 'Twin Peaks'. Anyway, the doll designer surely noticed it and mentioned it several times... 'that's an interesting beauty mark'.

After an hour of being dissected and studied, I was ready to wrap it up, book the job and move on to my next appointment in the city. Well, I had brought my carry-on suitcase to the agency and left it somewhere where the grouchy, older lady agent tripped and fell back over the bag. I ran over to help her up and apologized for her tripping over a stationary object! She was livid! Apparently, she had just recovered from hip surgery and she tripped over my bag! Oops! She banished me from ever representing me and didn't book me at the end for the 'Bratz Doll' unveiling at the 2001 Toy Fair. I left the office in tears!

Several months later, I came across a Bratz Doll at a toy store with a beauty mark under the left eye and caramel highlighted hair like me at the time. One side I was happy there was a doll that looked like me, and then on another side I had felt completely used. Every time, I see a Bratz Doll, I think about how I almost killed an old lady.

CHAPTER 8
HOCUS POCUS

I had an audition for a magician once. He was, I guess, a young David Copperfield. He was a medium height, slim built man with dark mysterious hair. I mean, mysterious by not sure how much hair gel this dude slapped on everyday, but dang! –mysterious. So, he was auditioning a female assistant for his shows. I thought this was perfect. It's like a showgirl secretary job without the typing and sitting at a desk, right? I can do that.

I went for two auditions for him- one of the auditions was at his Sutton Place apartment, which was lavishly decorated by an interior designer who was clearly a Liberace fan. It came down to me and another girl. Before I auditioned the second time for him, he told me his act was touring in Turkey for nine months. Ok, I have actually been to Turkey before when I was seven years old… and I do remember it being not so luxurious. Ok, for a seven-year-old to remember a place not being luxurious probably means it is a total dump. But I don't mean to trash an entire nation… I'm just recalling what I remember from my stay in Istanbul. With that memory and the fact that I would be separated from my cats, I decided I didn't want to go. So I messed up these extra cheesy dance moves in the name of not wanting to go to Turkey. And guess what?! It worked! He graciously let me know the news that he had chosen someone else and I was ecstatic!

I left the 2nd audition feeling like I had bit the bullet on that one. A nice, hot NYC pretzel was in order to celebrate that I wouldn't get my body cut in half by a flamboyant magician in Turkey!

CHAPTER 9
BOLLYWOOD… HERE I COME!

One of my jobs (Yes! I actually booked a job! So excited!... wait I have to dress like *what*?) took me to the lower East side to star in an Indian music video. Indian as in Bollywood Indian.

The singer was a twenty-something sweet, Indian man singing a long-winded ballad. They had us dressed in the most unsexy belly dancing costume on Earth. It was full of coins and jingly things, like a belly dancing costume, but they had tailored it to look 'modest'. As a matter of fact, I was covered head to toe with not a centimeter of skin showing, due to the censorship rules in India. They might as well have wrapped yards of sateen fabric around me right off the fabric roll and cinched it. I really didn't care because this belly dancer got paid $150 for the day! Okay, it was a Loooooong-ass day with lots of sweet, sweet dance moves around a pimped out Indian star, but I GOT PAID! Yes!!! I'm not sure if it aired in India, but it's always a great conversation starter to say you looked a fool in a music video that aired in a different country…. Trust me.

CHAPTER 10
CREDIT CARDS, PLEASE

So, I had a paper due in English class at college and I was in New York for the International Hair and Beauty show at the Jacob Javits Center. This was one of those conventions open to salon professionals and business owners looking for new techniques and products for hair.

Have you ever seen those superstar hairdressers on stage with dramatic rock-star music and lighting cutting and styling a model's hair on stage like it was a friggin' rock concert? Yeah, this is that. This is a show I would book every year (one year it was *Pureology*, another was *Sebastian*, etc) and it paid well considering the time I spent at the show and I would get an edgy haircut/color on top of it. This year, I had booked a gig modeling for *Paul Mitchell* on stage that year. I was doing the show for a weekend and was getting paid $500 and was getting a professional cut and color... or so I thought. However, as a demo model – the hair stylist is not obligated to 'finish' the process due to restricted time on stage. In other words, they will demonstrate on your hair on stage, but once the show is over, they'll leave your ass with an unfinished haircut and color. I later learned this was a clause in my contract that I had somehow missed.

So, they brought me onstage for all the hairdressers to learn a new coloring technique. They sat me down and started coloring my hair in a new technique called 'Credit Cards'. Anything credit card related sounds good to me! So, they started by frosting my hair to look like a checkerboard- a bleach blonde and black checkerboard to be exact! I could see time was running out and only HALF of my head was completed! The curtain dropped and I thought naively that the dude was going to finish my hair backstage. NOPE! He disappeared like a rockstar after the show and about two minions ran over and dragged my ass off stage to the back to wash out my hair. At this point, it still didn't sink in that they were done with my ass and that they just wanted to rinse me and send me off with a check. After the rinse, I was like 'So is anyone going to finish the color?'- the minions look at each other, cackled and walked away! I looked in the mirror... my head was a flippin' mess- half bleached, half black- it was like Cruella De Ville's hair after a flea bath.

One part humiliated, one part mad that my hair was fucked up, I quickly left with my check and ugly hair and bought a hat at a vendor on the way to the NY Public Library (remember I had a paper due?). I wrote my heart out on the steps of the library, which produced a D... I definitely had something else on my mind when I wrote that paper- my freshly fucked up hair!

CHAPTER 11
CHUCK E. SLEAZE

This one time I had to go for an audition in New Jersey. Huge mistake, I took a bus that took forever (Like two hours!). Naturally, the audition people didn't tell me how far away from the city they were, and I couldn't search it up online to see how far it really was... remember, pre-MapQuest days.

So, my journey began with a bus to New Jersey that stopped in front of a tired Chuck E Cheese. I was super hungry, so I went in and ate in the company of animatronic rodents and probably, real life rodents, too. The audition people arrived to pick me up. One looked like a straight up Meth face, the other I don't remember so clearly, so probably just normal. The other odd thing was that they had decided to bring their tabby cat for the ride, which was exciting for a cat lady like me.

Apparently, the cat would get car sick- and it did, right on my shoe! They were a pair of black leather platform boots that I had picked up in the East Village that soon became tainted with random cat vomit. The same boots my mother would chastise me for wearing for fear of me tripping and falling while crossing the street in NYC with no one to help me because I may have gotten a concussion from the fall. A little far fetched, but, yes, completely possible. The audition people said, 'sorry for that' and continued to drive with the sick cat. I was getting sick of this long ride and cat vomit.

Finally, we arrived. I read a few lines for them and then I was off back to the same Chuck E Cheese to catch the bus sent from heaven back to the city. From then on, I had decided no more auditions outside of the city. Also, I didn't get the part.

CHAPTER 12
A MAKE-SHIFT BOUDOIR

The port authority 2nd floor bathroom was my own boudoir. After a three hour ride on a bus, I would wash my face, brush my teeth, do my make up, do my hair, get dressed, take a baby wipe shower, rearrange my pocketbook, etc. I would go to into the city feeling fabulous, fresh and ready for my auditions and go-sees for the day. I would use it before my auditions and after all my auditions. I had everything perfectly placed on the counter, as to not pick up germs from the dirty bathrooms… It was like a science. People probably thought I was running an illicit makeup counter out of the bus station bathroom. Oh, if the mirrors and walls could talk…. Stop by there sometime… it still looks the same!

CHAPTER 13
SISTER BEAR

Not much of a story to tell, but I did dress up as a Berenstain Bear (Sister Bear) for their 40th anniversary celebration at The New York Public Library. We would greet kids and parents in the children's section, which was agonizing. Everyone knows a NYC kid is no ordinary kid. Most are diabolical and have an army of nannies to back them. They have a list of demands that need to be met and know how to strangle the competition with a quick pinch and evil side eye. And the parents will do whatever it takes to make their kid number one. Anyhow, inside the costume was sweltering, and I felt like I should've been paid more... thank god I had a mask over my head.

CHAPTER 14
PATRICIA FIELD

One of my favorite places in NYC was Patricia Field's. I had been shopping there since I was 13 or 1991. This was when they had a store on East 8th and Hotel Venus on West Broadway. My heart would skip a beat as I walked through the doors entering the world of kitsch, Harajuku style and drag queen emporium. All the one-of-a kind accessories and outfits from local and Japanese designers was like a burst of fresh air for me. This was before you could scroll on the internet… this was when you could actually feel and try on clothes and jewelry… I have to say about 60% of my closet currently is from Patricia Field's.

This was also an era when the club kids would work at the stores during the day. Amanda Lepore was the make up artist there and Richie Rich worked there, as well. A long tome friend of mine, Hushi used to work the counter and go under the moniker Hushi Robot. They've all come a long way in the fashion world- they all have their own thing going on.

I do remember trying to launch my own fashion line called *Mooshibear- Ready to Wear* and bringing a suitcase of my designs for the store buyer to look at. They didn't want to carry my line, but miraculously two weeks later, similar clothes like the ones I brought in were hanging in the store. I was a little disappointed, but not surprised.

Patricia Field's closed down their last store in 2014. I remember one of my last times at the store, I had brought my oldest son, who was at the time, two years old. He was completely mesmerized by the handsome, bearded African-American man in full drag behind the counter. Splendid memories and trinkets, calling an end to a fabulous era.

CHAPTER 15

BROOKLYN BOUND

This was before the New Jersey cat vomit incident where I had sworn never to leave the borough of Manhattan. I went for an audition in New Jersey again. It was an audition for the part of a lawyer in a movie. I got the part and showed up to the set in New Jersey a few days later. I had taken the bus to the location, however missed the last bus back into the city after the shoot.

The director was a smarmy guy, a good-looking, African American man with a penchant for Drakkar Noir and Adidas tracksuits, who was trying to lure me to his house to sleep overnight. There were subtle cues like putting his hand on my waist, the occasional brush of my hair off my face, a quick feel of my ass as I walked by that made me feel uncomfortable, especially since I was not really attracted to him. I think it was his sleazy disposition that was a turn–off.

The city was probably about 45 minutes away, so literally there was no need to sleep over a stranger's house ... it was only 6 pm. After many excuses of 'hitting traffic' and 'to just sleep over and then he'll take me into the city in the morning', I felt like he just wanted to get me alone and fuck. When it was apparent that his plans were foiled, he said 'You're a lost child... you need a man like me to guide you," and continued to make passes at me even after I clearly told him I'm not really interested.

Luckily, I met an actor (who looked like a young Robert Redford and lived in Brooklyn- more on that later!) on set that I had made aware of the situation and he took me back in his car to the city after the shoot.

Thank god for young Robert Redford... I believe he saved me from an awkward and potentially dangerous situation!

With all the #MeToo stuff going on, I can say that situation was pretty typical and run-of-the-mill back in my day. It was just expected, especially for a young, attractive girl trying to make it in the business. At times, I felt obligated and at times I felt infuriated. I guess it depended on how hot the guy was ... hahaha.

I commend the ladies who have spoken up about the experiences and hope future women know that it is your choice on how you want to navigate your way through the waters of the entertainment industry. I'm not saying that sexual favors must be eliminated... but rather, do what YOU want. If it is pleasurable for you and it may get you a part, why not?? If it's an uncomfortable situation, by all means, let yourself be heard by that person. The bottom line is communication. If you want to fuck the director, do it. If you don't want to, then tell him a firm 'no thanks' and move on. The power of a woman lies in getting what she wants on HER terms. So, if you're ever in a compromising situation, go with your gut and act on it.

That day, I went with my gut and got out of the situation. As for the young Robert Redford... we fucked later that night at his Brooklyn apartment. Young Robert Redford was an assistant at one of the top casting agencies in NYC. We kept in touch and would see each other sometimes when I was in town.

One night a blizzard hit Manhattan and left me stranded there. So, he took me to his place in Brooklyn. He had three other roommates. After a quick ride on the subway, I arrived to his apartment in Brooklyn and didn't realize it was a shady part of Brooklyn until when I left a few hours later in the wee morning hours. After a much needed romp in the bedroom or shall I say makeshift bedroom in the dining room (The rent is too damn high, folks!), he told me 'be careful walking to the subway' (which was a few blocks away) – I thought nothing of it until I saw a roving gang eyeing me. I took out my mace and brass knuckles, just in case. They didn't bother me, but I knew this was FOR SURE the last time I leave Manhattan. As Samantha would say from 'Sex and the City'...'I don't do boroughs'...words of wisdom, right there!

Chapter 16
TROMA-TIC STORIES

During my Troma days, Lloyd Kaufman hooked me up with some Israeli film makers that were making a campy horror movie called "Barbecue People". Okay, the name of that film just makes you want to run the other way... or go get baby back ribs. Anyway, seeing it was Lloyd that recommended the part, I accepted.

The shoot was in an old meat packing factory in Brooklyn. The morning of the shoot I arrive to the location by subway- it seemed deserted. It was an old brick factory with windows blown out, probably due to a shoot from a mafia deal gone sour. Okay, it probably just broke during storm or something. It's just me getting overly dramatic. Anyway, I double check the address... yep- this was it.

The odor of decomposing animal flesh wafted through the rickety front door... it was still a meat packing place on the first floor! Large hooks with animal carcasses were hanging in the locker room to the left. On the right, elevators... I choose the elevators. The place looked like scene out of American Horror Story. I take the huge commercial elevator upstairs and stumbled upon a sweat factory of fastidious Asian women sewing away without a batting an eye. I ask the manager if there was a film shoot in this building. He pointed towards a door in the back of the room. I made my way to the door that lead to a stairwell with a murder of dead crows with flies and maggots. At this point, I was totally creeped out and was pretty sure this is where I would die. This could've been a serial killer's office space for all I know! ...A very organized and precise serial killer, at least.

I reached the next floor door and had my mace ready, just in case. The film crew was there with all the actors. Whew! I went straight into makeup where they put a big, knife gash on my chest. The whole shoot took only a couple of hours and I earned my keep at $250. But did I die?? I didn't die. It was a good day.

CHAPTER 17
THE STONEY AWARDS

Another gig that Lloyd Kaufman hooked me up with were the 'Stoney Awards' in NYC. The awards are based on the accolades of marijuana in film and television. Now, I'm not a pot smoker, but have a lot of friends who do. But when you mix pot with say, a live show, well, things get a little crazy or shall I say very, very, very relaxed.

My part in the show was to present an award along with one of the writers of 'The Conan O'Brian Show' to the famed pothead duo, Cheech and Chong. We get on stage to present the award and literally, there was a large mushroom cloud of smoke hanging over the audience. It was impossible NOT to get a contact high in that place. I guess you could say that was the only time I experienced copious amounts of pot in my system, so my memory is a little fuzzy.

We presented the award to Cheech and Chong, who are some of the coolest dudes. It was a memorable, but not memorable evening to say the least...and I probably would do it again in a quick toke.

CHAPTER 18
FESTIVALS WITH TROMA

Part of being a Tromette was always having a free place to stay during The Cannes Film Festival in Cannes, France and during The Sundance Film Festival in Utah. It was a crazy ten days of non-stop partying and acting a fool on behalf of Troma on the French Riviera and also in the small Mormon town of Park City, Utah.

So, as soon as Lloyd would offer me a spot, I would snatch it up quickly. What fun it would be to frolic on the beaches of the French Riviera or be a snow bunny on the Utah mountains, while being serious about filmmaking! It was seriously just a bunch of crazy punks let loose in the stuffy business atmosphere of film markets... our presence was so controversial that we were banned from The Carlton Hotel in Cannes for life. The Carlton is probably one of the poshest, snootiest hotels in the world, so I don't really blame them for not wanting psycho, radical punks on their premises.

I had gotten there through Troma, but I had quickly learned that if I wanted to get further in the film industry, I was going to have to distance myself a bit from the constant circus called Troma. So, I went off on my own often during the Cannes Film Festival and Sundance Film Festival and networked with various people, including my future husband. I went a total of three times with Troma to Cannes and Sundance. Those were probably the craziest, fun-filled years of my life.

CHAPTER 19

TROMA'S EDGE TV

It was the day before Easter, and I was shooting an episode of Troma's Edge TV. Troma's Edge TV was a variety skit show of everything bizarre and campy starring the likes of Joe Fleishman, Julie Strain, Debbie Rochon, The Naked Cowboy and me. It was picked up for a full season by a network in England for their late-night line-up. We were scantily clad and sometimes topless, hence, the late-night TV slot.

After a full day of shooting at the Troma headquarters in Hell's Kitchen (a six-story, slender building right near The Amish Market) and with lots of gory special effects and cold pizza, I was feeling nauseas. It was super low budget, so the 'blood' was actually real blood from a butcher across the street. The smell was atrocious and the risk of staining my costumes frightened me.

I had driven myself there from RI with my red-headed friend, Heather, who lived in Connecticut and had a penchant for witchcraft, anything satanic and Aussie Spray Sprunch. We knew each other from the strip club we worked at in Rhode Island. Heather actually encouraged me to submit a headshot to Troma months before, which in turn got me a phone call for this gig. Being a very thankful and lovely friend, I brought her along to see if she could also have a part in the show. Also, I needed a bodyguard, in case shit got real. Heather was built like a voluptuous Amazonian woman who happened to be Irish, so this was definitely a win-win situation. The fiery temper of an Irish woman with the build of a gladiator was enough to ward off any kind of trouble.

So, we shot all day and into the early evening. I must have watched The Naked Cowboy devour, what seemed to be, 100 Slim Jims, 2 large bottles of Mountain Dew and 10 packs of Oscar Meyer Turkey slices. He was quite entertaining with his charming jingles and guitar riffs. In case you're wondering who 'The Naked Cowboy' is, he was a tall, buff guy from the South that would walk around playing guitar and singing country tunes around Times Square in nothing but his patriotic speedos and cowboy hat, even in the wintertime! He also had 'The Naked Cowboy' scribbled in blue glitter on his bare chest. He was a permanent fixture in Times Square during the late 1990s and early 2000s. You may have even spotted him a few MTV videos back in the day.

The crew from Troma wanted to go to a nightclub after the shoot to unwind and celebrate. Still feeling nauseas, we all go in my car and drive around. I started to feel really sick, so I asked Heather to drive, which is like a huge deal because my car at the time was like my baby. I even gave it an endearing name- 'Teutonic Terror'. Heather looked terrified because she didn't want to crash my BMW in the city, knowing that the car was my prized possession from my top sugar daddy of the moment, Tim. I insisted and so she drove precariously as I took a nap in the backseat. Miraculously, I felt better after a quick vomit out the window, but my car was starting to spew smoke from the under the hood. I'm sure it was a coincidence and it wasn't my friend's fault. My car and I were both feeling ill! It's crazy to say, but I believe I have an otherworldly connection with my car.

Anyway, we decided to park the car and go eat and deal with the car later. So, we went to Lucky Cheng's in the East Village. Lucky Cheng's is a drag queen institution serving Chinese fine dining with drag queen performers and waitresses. Okay, maybe not fine dining, but the sweet and sour chicken does taste better when a drag queen is giving your drunken friend a lap dance. Anyhow, after eating and partaking in shenanigans, I was feeling so much better! We come back to my car and see if my car started. It did! And it drove home all the way to Rhode Island! My car and I must have some kind of telepathy! Or Heather performed some kind of witchcraft hex to make the car drive... we'll never know!

CHAPTER 20
LA NOUVELLE JUSTINE

Speaking of NYC restaurant institutions, there was a very intriguing restaurant in lower Manhattan between Avenue A and B called 'La Nouvelle Justine' that I would visit often. It had a very unassuming entrance on the side of the street with a tiny picture frame of a very high heel with the name of the restaurant in elegant cursive. The whole thing was like an Eric Stanton drawing.

It was only open in the evenings and had a strict dress code of … fetish wear. This was a 4-star French restaurant with a fetish and bondage theme. It was the perfect date place, in my opinion. It was sort of my barometer in checking if a guy was daring or boring in bed. Nobody wants a dead fish in bed, right?? When you stepped into the cozy, dark, bustling restaurant, the first thing to catch the eye is the stage with a random person being flogged in leather bondage. Sometimes it was a hot busty chick and sometimes it would be a gay, hairy, leather daddy. You never knew what performance that night would be. Sometimes the waiters would give you a spank as they passed by with a tray of food.

It was hit or miss depending on your preferences. But what always seemed constant was the delicious steak frites and the life-sized chocolate high heel filled with berries and fresh whipped cream. The food was delightful and so was the entertainment. In 1998, 'La Nouvelle Justine' shut down due to a fire in a nearby apartment, which prompted the owners to open a new location called 'La Maison de Sade' in Chelsea… same theme , same menu… however, the neighbors had the place shut down in less than a year due to 'noise'... or as the neighbors claimed, 'evil' practices. Ha! Damn, I miss that place!

CHAPTER 21
FETISH MODELING

There was a husband and wife team of photographers that I had met in Providence when I was about 17 years old. I consider them my dear friends. They look like they were frozen during the hippy era and defrosted during the late 90's and early 2000. They had a studio in Providence in a dilapidated warehouse on Harris Ave. We collaborated on ideas naturally and made a very good team. I was into the David LaChapelle/FrenchVogue look and they were into the Eric Stanton/Helmut Newton sort of aesthetic. Together we created some very intriguing and fashion forward photos. I was very lucky to have met them because they shot 75% of my portfolio prior to 2005. Some of my most amazing vintage photos were shot by them.

Because of my love for corsets and my 50 plus custom corsets, they encouraged me to do fetish modeling to make a few bucks. I accepted and somehow this idea turned out to go from a few photoshoots to starting my own Fetish member's only website, *Persia's Boudoir*. This was in the late 1990s /early 2000, way before any burlesque or fetish became mainstream and popular. Also, the internet was new, so not many entertainers had websites yet, let alone paid members' websites. So, with no thought I decided to go for it.

Shortly after, I would attend Fetish conventions meeting other girls in the same business- performers like Dita Von Teese, Julie Strain and Masuimi Max. It didn't prove lucrative immediately, but had I stuck with it, I'm sure I would have made a hefty fortune. I didn't stick with it because I was newly engaged to my current husband and he understandably, didn't approve of it. And so, I hung up my corsets and stockings ...and fetish modeling had all been forgotten until about 15 years later (after having three children together).

My husband and I are now the photography team for my most recent shoots. As for the photographers who believed in me, I speak to the wife once in a while and the husband had sadly passed away from diabetes in 2019.

CHAPTER 22
TROY BOY

Providence is a very small city where everyone knows each other by probably one degree of separation, at most. I would frequent this club in the theater district called Club Hell. It was THE club in Providence. Each night was a different theme... Wednesday nights were Fetish nights; Thursdays were College Nights, etc. Depending on which night you went, you could either be rubbing shoulders with drunken college kids, or bumping into straightedge freaky, gothic misfits who drank water all night.

Anyhow, Club Hell and another place called Lupo's Heartbreak Hotel practically raised me since I was dancing my tiny ass off at the club since the age of 14, thanks to a fake ID. It was Club Hell where I did my first fashion show for Sarah Good Fashions and saw Green Day before they were a stadium band. As a matter of fact, my flirty encounter with Billy Joe of Green Day was one that would stay with me ... so much so that I ran into him YEARS later at Fred Segal on Melrose in LA and he damn recognized me and started talking to me! Tim the sugar daddy was with me at the time in the store and his face dropped when that happened. Anyhow, those were good times with good memories.

I also count Club Hell for introducing me to my first real boyfriend who was eight years older than me, Troy, a tall, slim guy with Japanese flower sleeve tattoos on both his arms, shaved head, side chops, goatee and a 'Prince Albert'. A Prince Albert for those of you not in the know is a ring piercing through the hole of the penis. It is for optimal sexual pleasure and I can vouch for that! Troy was a small-time drug dealer that had a paralegal job during the day at one of the big law firms downtown. He was a perfect gentleman. He was the right balance of punk and businessman.

At the time he was running 'Swing Night' at Club Hell on a Tuesday nights. This was back when Swing music and everything rockabilly was all the rage. I had gotten all dolled up in black Capri pants and a gingham button down shirt tied at the midriff. My hair was done up in a 1950s headscarf with pin curls. He was dressed in a green 1950s suit with black detailing... the kind of detailing you might find on a bowling ball or something. Anyway, he caught my eye from across the dance floor and when they say 'Love at First Sight'... man! It was ... love at first sight. I was so enamored by the way he handled everything and how he carried himself and how he was the boss.

Later that night, he tracked me down and introduced himself. He asked me where I worked and to not fuck it all up, I lied and said I was a waitress at a club. Ok, so I guess lying right off the bat is technically fucking things up. Of course he asked me which club, to which I lied again! I said Lupo's... He looked at me all suspicious... he said he'd never seen me there before and how his friend owns the club, blah blah blah. Shit. I left it at that, and he asked me out to dinner a for Thursday night. I was squealing inside but gave a non-excited yes! But, yes...I was so excited! We exchanged beeper numbers (beepers were THE thing back then...) and that was that.

I remember later that night I was sitting in front of the mirror all giddy getting ready for bed when I said to myself that I would marry Troy one day. I really believed it. I was so smitten, but knew I had to come up with a story about where I worked before Thursday. I had two days to come up with a story about working in a club and make it believable to guy or knows EVERY SINGLE club within a 45 mile radius.

Thursday rolled around quickly ... we met at a restaurant on the East side of Providence and had lovely conversation and dinner. We had a lot of friends in common and had the same taste in music and fashion. He was a lot like a gay straight guy, if that makes any sense. He was into fashion, but still had a masculine sex appeal about him and he was straight! That combination is really hard to find, by the way... either a dude is up on fashion totally a friend of Dorothy's or they're the typical football watching, beer drinking Neanderthal with no interest in art and fashion, but totally into pizza and chicks. I felt like I had stumbled upon a rare unicorn with Troy.

Anyhow, the inevitable came... so, are you really a waitress at a club?? He knew I was lying, and he knew I knew he knew. So, I came clean... fuck it, right...? So, I told him I was a stripper going to college. He was eight years my senior, so I'm sure the college girl thing turned him on in any case. He laughed a bit and said he already knew and had asked some friends about me... he even knew what club I worked at. I felt relieved and went continued at ease on our first date. We talked and talked and laughed and laughed... it was truly one of my best dates ever easily and we barely went anywhere except dinner and then out for drinks at a place called Jerky's, just upstairs from Club Hell. It was his main hang out and was tight friends with the owner.

Troy was a man about town. Everyone knew him wherever we went. He was protective, sweet, and in charge... everything I look for in a man. He didn't mind me dancing, I had asked him not to come in to visit me because I didn't know how he would handle other guys looking at me and what not. So, that was our little pact.

I invited him on a two-day cruise to Nova Scotia with my school to get to know him a bit better. They always say, travel with a lover to find out that person's temperament. The cruise was really a big blur thanks to my gay friend Jimmy. He offered us Tic-Tacs, which were really pot pills. Naturally, we each had 3-4 'Tic-Tacs', before we felt the onset of, basically, having our heads up our asses for two days straight. Thankfully, the cruise had a mini casino and we gambled the days away. On our downtime, we tried to fuck in our prison cell of a room on the boat while still high on pot pills and seasickness. Not a good combo.

The morning of our arrival back to land, the effects of sea nausea and pot pills were waning, and we decided to go back to Troy's Victorian apartment in Providence. I gave him a proper blowjob and went on my merry way to school. It was a pretty good weekend, except I felt without the pills and seasickness; it could've been better. Also, Jimmy's advances towards Troy were getting to be annoying.

See, Jimmy thought Troy was gay, but then again Jimmy thinks every man I dated had gay tendencies. He would try to lure them to the gay side and report to me if they were full on hetero or not. Anyway, Jimmy's tactics were most always entertaining It wasn't until years later that I found out that Troy is in fact bisexual. So, Jimmy was actually on to something. But at the time, I had brushed it off as Jimmy's way of attention whoring away from my boyfriend.

Troy and I continued to see each other... we had lovely conversation and preferred to have a quiet dinner and night in since we both worked in the nightclub industry. Our relationship was heavily reliant on sex. We would fuck anytime, any place, listening to Massive Attack, while watching Howard Stern on TV, you name it. We were both sexually attracted to each other in a crazy way. It was the kind of sex that would inspire porn scenes and long-winded, soft porn, romance novels. Some of the best sex I had ever had was with Troy. When he would cum, his Prince Albert would split it into two streams... it was comical, yet hot. We had sex with condoms mostly, but quickly would just forgo the condom and did the pull-out method.

Every month I would pray for my period to come since I felt wasn't ready for a baby, yet. Troy was the type of guy that could move on to another girl easily. And to add to the mayhem, me as a dancer who moves on to another guy easily business-wise, would make for a volatile relationship.

We must've broken up and gotten back together a million times during the two years we were together. Each time, we would try to spite each other by showing off a new lover around town. Of course, deep down I really wanted it to work with him. We had so much in common, but he was so afraid of commitment. I didn't want to get married or anything, I just wanted us to be exclusive ... that's all. I had even started birth control to show him I trust him to be exclusive with me.

My mom HATED Troy. He met my mom and brother early in our relationship and although he put on a pretty good act for them, my family thought of him as a 'loser' mainly because he wasn't a doctor. That's the Persian view on life. If you're not a doctor, you are a loser. Makes ZERO sense.

Anyway, the first time he met my mom and brother (my dad was out of the picture already... we were estranged, and he was somewhere in California) we had lunch on the deck at our house in Smithfield. Troy would give hilarious bullshit stories, like 'I enjoy watching National Geographic and C-Span during my leisure times." HAHAHAHAH! The dude watched Howard Stern and the Playboy Channel regularly. Or "I enjoy my work as a paralegal and would like to one day become a lawyer. " HAHAHAHA! Dude was a drug dealer and after -hours rave organizer with the Paralegal as his cover job. My family smelled the bullshit and hated him. The tattoos and piercings didn't help either. I had frequent fights with my mother about sleeping over at Troy's apartment several times a week. I was over 18 and she was still trying to tell me what to do. I was furious.

    I ended up telling her that I have invited Troy for Thanksgiving dinner with us in Newport. My mom was livid! I ended up not go to Thanksgiving and spending it alone with Troy at his apartment (he barely had any family, he considered a dive bar, Jerky's to be his family). I told him about how my family felt about him and it was pretty much the beginning of our constant break ups for the next year and half. We ended up having AMAZING make-up sex every time.... the kind where people would gather at the window to hear all the moans and groans.

    As a matter of fact, one summer night we had just come back from going out and we had the loudest sex at, like, 3 am at his apartment. He lived on the first floor with his bedroom window right near the sidewalk. After our loud sex, we noticed some whispering and giggling outside... a crowd of about 6-7 of his college -aged neighbors were gathered outside listening to us fuck and talk dirty. It was slightly embarrassing, but also a little bit like a performance. Anyhow, sex was the one and pretty much only thing that was keeping us together.

My job at the strip club bothered him and I wasn't about to quit, especially because it was around the time when Tim the sugar daddy was about to buy me a car. It didn't help that his friends would tell him they had spotted me with one of my clients at a restaurant or shopping either. Our relationship had taken a toll and neither of us wanted to budge, so after two years, we parted ways in the worst possible way.

My suspicion of him seeing other girls was confirmed with a friend seeing the girlfriend of his best friend leaving his apartment one morning. Obviously, they had fucked. That was the final nail in the coffin. I was a sordid wreck. Going out in Providence would never be the same... running the risk of run into him and his friends was enough to make me sob in public. I was not about to have that!

So, my new policy on boyfriends was, have fun, but focus on business at the club, which I did even though it was painful inside. I never had so many regular clients and making so much money ever in my life. I was living the Glamorous Life with money and furs... who needs a boyfriend? On the outside I had it all....on the inside, I was broken and wounded. It was time to numb myself and move on. Last I heard Troy was part owner (partners with Chef Boy, the one that I had diddled while we were on a break) of a popular bar in Brooklyn. Cheers to that.

CHAPTER 23
WALL STREET GUY

There was a dark-haired, thirty-something Wall Street Guy in NYC that I was dating. His office was in the World Trade Center South building. He was an attractive, relatively young fellow that I had met at a strip club in midtown called 'Scores'. I don't know what my attraction to him was... he was good looking in my book, but we never 'clicked'. He was a little self-absorbed and gave me Christian Bale in 'American Psycho' vibes, but actually was not psycho, at all, just mega boring, especially for a Quaalude popping, coke-sniffing Wall Street dude.

For a girl like me, anyone psycho would not be someone I'd like to tangle with unless I wanted to be the headlining news on 'A Current Affair'. Come to think of it, I had a lot of potential "A Current Affair" moments, but I'd like to think my street smarts helped me avoid those bad situations throughout my life.

I do remember his Upper West side apartment. He happened to live across the hall from the MTV host at the time, Carson Daly. His family lived in South Hampton and they were Jewish. Not an orthodox Jew, but enough Jewish to date a non-Jewish girl not so seriously. I am a non-Jewish girl; therefore, I was in the fling category... definitely not someone to take home to Mom in the Hamptons.

I really didn't care- he had an impeccably clean and tidy apartment, a nice view of Manhattan facing south on the upper west side and was virtually never home. On the downside, his fridge was empty always, except for a few cartons of Ceres juice (which I drink to this day because of his introduction to this great brand of juice), wore running clothes on our first date, and was meh in bed.

In the beginning of our relationship because he would work until about 6 or 7 pm, we would meet around 8 or 9 for dinner and then cruise around Manhattan in his brand-new Porsche 911. By the way, if you can fuck in a Porsche 911, you deserve a goddamn trophy. The car is so compact and tiny, almost claustrophobic. So, that witching hour between 6pm and 8pm, I roamed the streets of NYC with achey feet from walking around and going to auditions and go-sees all day. So, I would restaurant hop during those in-between hours because a) the shops were closed and b) the shops were closed. Also, I was tired as fuck. So, because of this I was forced to eat and never be hungry for our date. He must have thought I was anorexic or something. I'm sure he didn't mind since I was pretty much a cheap date.

One of our dates was on a Friday night and he wanted to 'beat the traffic' to the Hamptons. So, he untied me from the bedpost after an uninspiring sex session and proceeded to pack his shit and went down to load his Porsche while I got dressed. I knew it was the last time I would see him… I didn't want to keep going for the sake of bad sex, access to his nice apartment, and boring Wall Street-related conversations (which actually, I learned a lot from). If I was going to be with someone so goddamn boring, at least give me the key to your apartment, so I can chill and drink your fancy juice while you're not there!

Anyway, in the end I wasn't disappointed …. we realized we virtually had nothing in common. He liked Bob Dylan and I liked Bjork. Months after we stopped seeing each other, 9/11 happened. I called him to see if he was okay. It was an awkward phone call- but he was okay, and we ended up asking each other where we were on that fateful day. He had miraculously missed the event due to him driving home late from the Hamptons and planning on going to the office later that day. Whoever he was fucking in the Hamptons saved his life. We spoke quickly to check in and made sure each of us were okay. We were both okay and life resumed. ...And that was the end of that.

CHAPTER 24
CHEF BOY

My ex-boyfriend, Troy, from Providence had a friend who was a chef in Manhattan. He lived in Brooklyn and was very gracious in letting me stay at his apartment once when I had an actor's convention to go to in NYC. It was a cold and blustery day in the city and Chef Boy was getting off work at 8pm. He told me to meet him at the subway entrance of Prince Street on Broadway. And so, I stood there in my luxurious fur coat, as he emerged from the other side of the street subway and whisked me away from the cold to the subway below.

It was a bit awkward because at this point, my ex and I had already split for the 1st time (we got back together a record 4 times!) It wasn't my first-time meeting Chef Boy, but it was the first time we were alone. We got off at Williamsburg and took a cab to his apartment. At this point, he had been up since 6am. We went to his humble abode and I gave him chocolates that I had bought from a drug store as my token of appreciation. In hindsight, I realize drug store chocolates are not gifts to give to a rising pastry chef star, especially one who was working with Michelin rated Jean-Louis Palladin. He accepted with genuine gratitude and asked me if I wanted to go out to a night club.

We engaged in witty banter, watched the Food network (which at that time I was first introduced to the Iron Chef) and slowly got ready to go out clubbing. We went to a gritty bar near the Port Authority and then to The Roxy. We had great conversations along the way and enjoyed each other's company. When it was time to retire at the apartment, I wanted to sleep on the couch, but he insisted on me sleeping in his bed.

It was a very cold night. I accepted naively thinking I would sleep on one side and he on the other . Well, I was wrong. We really liked each other and although it wasn't a 'home run', let's say it was 3rd base. I felt a little guilty about him being my ex's best friend. Morning came around and things changed. It was a new workday, and Chef boy had to go to work very early in the day.

As we left the house, he was listening to his phone messages when he said his girlfriend had called a left a message. Midway through the voicemail, he DELETES her message. First off, there never was a mention of a girlfriend and he disrespects her by deleting her halfway through her message?! That's when I realized dysfunction runs in herds. I never heard from him after and it wasn't until years later I saw him on a bus from NYC to Providence with his girlfriend. He didn't recognize me, and I didn't bother to remind him. Today, I read about him occasionally in Bon Appétit and other food magazines.

CHAPTER 25
LOFTY GOALS

I was dating this guy from NY who was much older than me- 30 years to be exact. He had a great loft apartment right in the middle of Union Square. I have to be honest; the loft apartment was the deal maker! I could care less about the guy. He ran a scam of a film festival thriving off of people trying to make it in the film industry. I had met him one year at the Cannes Film Festival when I had traveled with Troma. I ended up crashing at his hotel suite at the Noga Hilton for two weeks.

One day, I was coming back to his apartment after a day of shopping and stepped into the elevator. A guy from my past was standing there. It was a guy who had shot my first photo shoot in Providence at his studio on Angell Street. I was barely 17 during the photo shoot. I was looking to build my portfolio and we agreed on a trade deal to build each others portfolios. He was a very talented photographer and shot some of my best photos to this date.

However, he became my stalker. How do I know this? He would call my house (I was living with my family, mind you) and ask for me and start breathing heavily and not talk. He would do this several times a day for about two months. Finally, during one of these calls, I heard his makeup artist saying hi to him. That's when he hung up and I finally knew who that was. I confronted him over it, and he denied it. One of his friends was my acquaintances and said that he had photos of me all over his bedroom. He said he felt inclined to tell me.

So, I see this man in the elevator in my boyfriend's apartment building in NYC four years later. Apparently, he shot for FHM magazine occasionally and his studio was in that building. Strange how people cross paths. Stranger how strange people get far in life. We both recognized each other, but rode the elevator in silence.

Back to the rich, scam artist boyfriend... his loft apartment in Union Square was amazing. I would spend a few days there at a time, scheduling auditions, going shopping and just living as a New Yorker at the expense of my older boyfriend. I remember he had a fish tank in his apartment that hid a giant safe. In the safe were stacks of cash. Every time he would take me out on the town, he would go to the tank, feed the fishes and then open the safe and take a wad of cash. It was like an aquatic ATM. So fascinating. I never talked about money, I would rather not know how people make their money, but I knew something was a little fishy... like, literally, I bet that cash smelled fishy.

Anyway one night, it was the opening of his shoddy film festival at Madison Square Gardens. I had planned on attending the opening and then driving back home to Rhode Island later that night, since I had my once-a-month mandatory day shift at the strip club and one of my clients was visiting. I knew something was up when he was giving me the cold shoulder all night. I realized he had been eyeing another girl at the party. This was a girl I had seen here and there at his loft/office area. I put two and two together and left the opening and met up with a few friends. Fuck That dude! He was old, getting stingy and I was tired of his laissez-faire attitude when it came to our relationship. Also, I had this other Wall Street guy on and off on the side, anyway.

So later that night, I met up with a couple of friends and had late-night breakfast at the IHOP in Times Square. It's now closed, but was a hotspot back in the day. I remember ordering waffles and regretting it after seeing a rat run across the kitchen floor. I had already put Scam Guy behind in my mind and was ready to just move on... I had a great night with friends and a belly full of waffles, strawberries and whipped cream before I headed home to RI later that night... that would be the last night before NYC would change forever. The next day, 9/11 happened.

    I was sitting at in my boudoir doing my hair and makeup for my day shift at The Foxy Lady after a late-night drive home, when the radio announced the first tower and then the second tower being hit. I, literally, was shaking... I had just been there hours before. I couldn't get a hold of anyone for weeks because the telephone lines were down. The days coming had been surreal like in a post-apocalyptic film. I went into work dazed and sat with my client, Jack, all day glued to the TV.

CHAPTER 26

FOX FORCE FIVE

I auditioned for a girl band on the same day that I was doing a fashion show for 'Clutch Fashions' later that evening. It was a warm spring afternoon in 1997. I auditioned somewhere in midtown Manhattan and got the part on the spot. It was Dee Snider's manager (The lead guy from the best rock band ever- 'Twisted Sister') and this poppy girl, Lisa, who were trying to put together a Spice Girl's type of pop band.

The deal was for all of us (five girls) to live in a house to get used to each other and starting writing material and rehearsing. We were called 'Fox Force Five ', named after the fictitious Charlie's Angel –type show from *Pulp Fiction*. So, based on that we had to be five girls. There were two girls who never came to practice and never moved in…. so, I guess technically, we were only three. Also, to be in a girl band, you could totally get away with doing absolutely nothing except look good because, honestly, do you really need FIVE people to sing a damn pop sing? Really? So, our phantom members were just that… two fillers that would show up for photoshoots and shows and just wing it.

Also, I was pleased that I was part of a girl group instead of alone, where music producers could really take advantage of you, like that one time a music producer in a wheelchair asked me to give him a hand job in return to the rights of a song he had written. I left that audition in tears, by the way. Or the time a 70 year old guy in the music business lured me to his apartment to his 'recording studio' in his bedroom and pulled down his pants and said he'd make me a star just after a quick blowjob. I also ran away in tears that day.

Anyway, I would spend the weekdays in Elizabeth, New Jersey and the weekends in Rhode Island dancing at my regular job as a career exotic dancer. Yes, I took that job seriously and am still living off that money! Coincidentally, my medical student brother was doing a rotation at a hospital in Patterson, just 20 minutes away. A very strange coincidence for a couple of kids from Rhode Island.

I was really excited and went and got all sorts of inflatable Hello Kitty Furniture from Target for my one room in the shared house in Elizabeth, NJ. It was an adventure! I have to say, Elizabeth was really a dumpy place, but it wasn't that far from the NYC. I had decided to get an evening job for when we weren't rehearsing at Score's night club in NYC. It was only a 45-minute train ride each way and it was a good way to earn some extra money in a different market than RI and also escape the mundane house of pop and inflatable Hello Kitty furniture back in Jersey. I met a lot of hot, yet sleazy Wall Street men who I would later end up dating here and there.

Back to Fox Force Five.... we really never got around to writing anything and we didn't get along after a month for some reason. The two other girls in the house were that poppy girl, Lisa, that was running the audition, who was unnaturally obsessed with this new site called eBay and this doe-eyed, black girl with a great voice (we'll call her Aretha). I don't really remember the other two girls since they were never there.

One day I arrived at the train station from RI and Aretha picked me up and said Lisa was talking behind my back about how she wants me out of the band. Now, I don't mean to toot my horn, but I had a fabulous wardrobe and more 'star quality' than Lisa... Aretha had sheer talent with a strong voice and a cute face, but Lisa? She was like a peppy, pop version of MTV's Daria with a debilitating addiction to eBay and faux, high-ponytail hair extensions. So, eBay was not even a year old... it was a new concept at the time and personally, I thought it was probably a scam. I would rather buy stuff at a real store in the East Village.

Strange things started happening at the house, like having items mysteriously disappear and then reappear after asking everyone if they had seen the item. My tea kettle melting on the stove when I wasn't even making tea....Or scratching noises at my door late night and no, we did not have a CAT! And the worst offense, using my makeup without my permission! Blasphemy!

Anyway, I think ultimately Lisa didn't want to share the spotlight and it was proven when she had told Aretha that I'd be better off doing my own thing. Honestly, it was a relief. I was more punk –rock and they were more R&B, radio edit pop. Traveling to NJ every week, being isolated in a house in the middle of a factory town, cutting back on hours at my regular club in RI, and dealing with and members with no motivation was taking a toll on me. The whole thing lasted all but three months.

I think the only time we went out as a band was to one of Dee Snider's concerts at a high school gym in a nearby dreary New Jersey town. Our manager wanted us to dress up as Fox Force Five to create a buzz. I distinctly remember the air of jealousy from Lisa getting ready in the bathroom that night. It was like she was studying me, but also throwing daggers with her eyes. At the concert, people were oohing and awww-ing over my hot pink fur coat, spiked collar, black vinyl thigh high platform boots and a face dipped in silver glitter. I was more KISS, than Spice Girls. The other two girls looked liked they had walked out of a Contempto Casuals catalog.

    Later on, she had ordered some things off of eBay that was clearly my style. Biting my style AND being psychotic? I ain't got time for that! So, I called my brother and asked him to pick me and my plastic hello kitty furniture up and take me back to RI ASAP. He did without question… a few hours later he showed up in his little, blue MiniCooper rescuing his little sister. I never seen or heard from those girls again, although I do wonder if Aretha ever got any gigs singing. And that is the story of the most short-lived girl band in history- Fox Force Five.

CHAPTER 27
CLUB KID

The late 1990s were the hey-days for the Club Kids of NYC. If you've ever seen "Party Monster' with Macaulay Culkin, (great film, by the way) you can see one viewpoint of the club kid life and the true story of the murder of 'Angel' at the hand of a tweaked-out Michael Alig. The crazy thing is that I used to go to Michael Alig's parties at The Limelight and The Tunnel. I had acquaintances with James St. James and Amanda Lepore and a few other club kids, mostly ones that worked at Patricia Field's during the day. I am still in touch with James St. James, who now lives in Hollywood and works for World of Wonder. Amanda still lives in NYC and shares an apartment complex with another friend of mine, Jeffrey.

This was pre-9/11 NYC; post Studio 54, where things were wild, uninhibited and personal expression came by way of outrageous costumes and makeup. The club kids were even featured on The Sally Jessie Raphael Show!

The parties were super original.... A bath foam party, where enormous amounts of bath foam was all over the dance floor, then there was a serial killer party, bloody everything, then there was the infamous impromptu rave at the Times Square McDonald's (I was there!). I wasn't into drugs, but I definitely admired everyone's costume and I loved to dance. I preferred NYC to Providence nightclubs, just for the WOW factor of it all. Everything was 100 times more extra in NYC than in Providence.

One of my friends had an extra ticket to go see Massive Attack at the Avalon in Boston. I had never really partied in Boston. Honestly,

Boston is a really conservative city and it really had no appeal to me except for shopping here and there on Newbury Street. But Massive Attack!? Yes, please! I had just gone through a shitty breakup (for the millionth time) with Troy and my first Persian cat, Felfel, had just died. I was looking to just go out and have fun and forget all about it. So, I took up my friend on the offer. Avalon was Boston's biggest nightclub (at least at the time) and is located right behind Fenway Park. If you're ever in Boston, ask someone to say 'Storrow Drive', just for shits and giggles. It will most likely sound like 'Stir-O dwive' with the Boston accent- highly entertaining to hear. Anyway, we went to the show and were front row. Massive Attack is a very cool trip hop band that you must hear at some point, if you have never. Groundbreaking music. Also, ideal music for tantric sex.

 So, after the show, a guy in a suit came up to me and asked me if I'd like a job. A job doing what? I hope not a blowjob, because seriously I was dressed super unsexy and club kid style ... like a cross between Bjork and Lady Miss Kier. I had my hair in pigtails with Shirley Temple curls, a sheer Jean Paul Gaultier dress with Ganesh printed on it, an orange Muppet fur shrug and big ass black platform shoes. If that didn't scream "RIOT GIRL THAT WILL CUT YOUR DICK OFF", then I don't know what will. Anyway, the guy in the suit was the manager of not only Avalon, but also the two smaller clubs next door The Monkey Bar and something else that was more like a dive bar. His name was Eric B and he was super polite, yet curt. I was so delighted and flattered that the biggest nightclub in Boston wanted me to work for them that I said yes on the spot. I didn't even know how much I was making, what nights, and what the hell my job was. All I knew was that I wanted to bring a bit of NYC club kid to Boston, because everyone knew that boring city needed some excitement!

Later on, we ironed out the details... I would be working the door on Friday nights at The Monkey Club, a chill lounge next door to the Avalon and then, some Fridays I would switch and work the VIP area inside of Avalon. He gave me a list of people to let in and not let in... let in was celebrities, hot couples, guys with nice clothes, and always, always let in hot chicks. Don't let in crack heads, people with ripped clothing, anything that resembles a hobo and no nerdy guys. Basically, it was a lounge for beautiful people. As for the VIP area at Avalon... that was easy, I went by the list they gave me, with the occasional celebrity. One night Dido came in with some friends, then one of the Wahlberg's, who was not Marky Mark came in, and a few others. It was a pretty fun gig.

I could wear whatever I wanted, the pay was good, but the commute sucked. I had to drive through Boston traffic on a Friday night, while they were still doing the Big Dig construction- tunnels of highway built underneath the city. This one night I almost literally drove off a bridge! Apparently, the construction people had forgot to block off an area leading to a bridge that was halfway built over a river. I drove and drove and realized the bridge had ended halfway! That would've been the night I thanked my lucky stars for being sober enough to notice.

The Boston job was another fun experience for me. I ended up meeting and dating this generic Boston guy for a few months. He turned out to be exactly as expected boring and unoriginal. Plus, the distance, just didn't even work. So, that was that and eventually, the Boston gig had run its course. School had started up again and I needed to focus on my final year in college, plus, I had joined a punk band, The L.U. V's, that demanded my time.

CHAPTER 28

PUNKS NOT DEAD, IT JUST GOT MACED

During the late nineties, I was in several local bands... mostly glam punk. One was a short-lived punk band called 'Hawaii', which I don't think we even got around to recording or playing in public. It was mostly short-lived because of our antics off-stage, like the time our concert poster had images of BDSM, and we unknowingly put it up in area of our college that also housed a daycare and elementary school. Oops. We got into hot water for that, but no worries, all of the members of Hawaii regrouped and changed our name to 'The L.U.V.s", which we ended up recording two full-length albums "Hate to Sleep Alone" and 'Stay Pretty'.

The band was a bunch of my guy friends... Miguel Souza (aka Johnny Velour) on vocals (*side note: Miguel and I had a college radio show together called 'The Roxy and Johnny Velour Show" for a few years... good times!*), Kevin Bowden (aka Billy Metropolis a celibate Prince fan) on guitar, Joshua Livingston (Vinyl Ricci) on bass and Paul DeVernais (aka Paul D) on drums. I did background vocals and was the resident go-go dancer, of course.

We played local nightclubs regularly in and around Providence and Boston and even had won WBRU's 'Rock Hunt' contest in 1997. We also ventured and played in Connecticut and NYC, including the lesbian dive bar, Meow Mix. Those were some wild times and can say that I'm really proud of the music.

After our wildly popular first album, we got the opportunity to go tour and open for major label band, Orgy. Orgy had a one hit wonder back in 1998 called "Blue Monday'. It was actually a hard-core cover of a

New Order song. Well, not really that hard-core if it was played on conventional radio stations and on high rotation on MTV... which it was. It was a huge song. Nonetheless, we were flipping ecstatic opening for them. Except, there was a kink in all of it... the lead singer, Miguel, decided to marry and stay home with his girlfriend/future ex-wife, Sherrie. I'm not sure of the details, but it was pretty standard, it's me or the band kind of stuff... and Miguel chose her. The rest of us in the band were pretty pissed to piss away such a fantastic opportunity. We all had been waiting for the moment to take our band to the next level and well, Sherrie, shit on all of that. Thank you, Sherrie.

Anyway, after all that hoopla, the band was a bit out of sorts and not in sync. There was a lot of animosity and bass player Josh aka Vinyl Ricci had a new skanky girlfriend, Jenny LaHurricane, that was clawing her way into also becoming a go-go dancer / background vocalist. I couldn't stand her... she was too Sid & Nancy to me... even hygiene-wise. It was a classic tale of fuck a band member and get in the band. I have to say, even though I may look like I sleep with anything that moves, the truth is that I actually never have slept or fooled around with anyone of the band members. I was always the funny, little sister type to them, so to be ravaged by a true sleazy skank hoping to replace me was a kick in the stomach.

In any case, I did remain civil even though I fucking hated her guts... the overdrawn raccoon eyes, the scrappy short bleach blonde hair, the ripped fishnets at least were a stark contrast to my 1960s James Bond silhouette girl look. My look was pretty much a 1960s bouffant, cat eyeliner and a latex/PVC catsuit.... Very *"Austin Powers"* or better yet, *"Faster Pussycat- Kill Kill Kill"* .

So, the band decided it would be a good idea that they have both of us as go-go dancers during a show at The Met in Providence. We were playing for a sold-out crowd and die-hard fans. The scene was mostly punk rock teenagers, some rockabilly heads and a lot of ska fans. Oh, and tons of screaming lady groupies for Johnny Velour, of course ... aka a recently engaged Miguel. Miguel looked something like a young Portuguese Johnny Depp at the time. We used to call him the 'Portuguese Prowler' because of his ability to swoon the girls just enough to buy the album, but not enough to be marked as a cheater to his future wife. Although I can appreciate his hotness, he became nothing more than a big brother to me more than anything... that, including the fact that I resembled his real-life little sister.

Anyway, back to the fateful night at The Met.... It was a packed Friday late spring night in 1998. Colleges were in the swing of prepping for finals and graduations and the crowd just wanted to let some steam off... including me. I was at a boiling point with Jenny LaHurricane's antics and the fact that the band wasn't backing me up. It was near the end of our set when we were coming back to the stage for our encore. Remember Sherrie, Miguel's fiancé who derailed our tour with Orgy? She pulls me aside and tells me that guitarist Kevin Bowden aka Billy Metropolis was giving me the middle finger the whole time between riffs and sets. That was it. It pushed me over the line. I grabbed my mace, went back on stage and maced the shit out of Bowden's face.

Mayhem ensued in the small, dingy nightclub. People were starting to fight each other, running out of the club, still moshing etc., etc. As soon as I did it, I left the club and came across some Providence cops at the corner. They asked what had transpired. I kindly explained that I maced a guy that was bothering me. They looked at each other, laughed and let me go endearingly... that's Providence cops for you, by the way. Punk, hood-rat stuff is mere child's play in a city run by the mob. At least they know, priorities! I quickly drove away and was thinking, this is it... end of an era... not only did I lose my band, but I lost friends, or at least what I thought were my friends. I heard through the grapevine that Billy Metropolis has in bed with eyes swollen shut for nearly a week. I also heard through the grapevine that he was planning on putting a hit on me. Let's just say after that night, I knew exactly who my friends were.

The band put out one more album after that without me, but the breakup of Jenny LaHurricane and Josh Vinyl Ricci was the last nail in the coffin. The band broke up and dispersed. I focused on my exotic dancing and expanding my business into my boss's 2nd new club in Massachusetts and the others went off and ended up getting married or working normal jobs.

I was still determined to get into music somehow, so I put an ad in the local paper for an electronic music producer. This time I wanted to be my own boss, controlling the music, my look and how I distribute. That's when I met a Brazilian guy named Eddie. Eddie was a freakishly tall man, with amazing computer, music producing skills. It was just the two of us and I was in charge of writing lyrics and hooks. We managed to put out an album called 'Anjos Burning', which went nowhere.

So, what does Anjos mean? Funny story... I asked him to call it Angel's burning, except his accent got in the way and he wrote 'Anjos'. I didn't realize this until 1000 copies of CD's had arrived with 'Anjos Burning'.

At first, I was livid... how can we promote an album with such a fucked-up typo!? Then, Eddie made it perfectly clear... 'anjos' means 'angels' in Portuguese. FUCKING BRILLIANT!!! At least it means SOMETHING in some language. So, our ass was saved. So, if you come across a Portuguese titled album with my name on it.... You know why. So random! It was time to move on from Eddie and find a new music producer with more of an alternative edge. You see, Eddie was more of a guido, techno kind of music producer. Not that there's anything wrong with that, but I was looking for more like a Garbage, Luscious Jackson sort of sound, so once again I put an ad in the local paper.

This time, it turned out to be an exciting adventure that produced absolutely no music...

CHAPTER 29

BARNES AVENUE BOYS CLUB

We were upon the 21st century (year 2000) and I was ready for a fresh new look, new career direction and just being my own boss. I had moved on to another strip club in Providence called The Foxy Lady, since Mario's had shut down. My former boss of five years had decided to sell the club and move his operation to Tennessee and Massachusetts, so I decided to part ways and stay in Providence. I had already owned some properties and had a nice investment package going with my stripper money that I had accumulated over the years. It was time for me to really pursue my dreams and really dive into acting and music. So, I put out an ad for an electronic producer to help me cut my second electronic/pop album.

This was around the time when Alice Deejay and Daft Punk ruled the club scene and that was exactly what I had in mind for myself. A lanky tall guy in his mid 20's named Matt answered the ad. I met him at his Victorian House rental on the East Side of Providence that he shared with four other roommates. There was Dan, a chubby, smooth talking emcee with a fun sense of humor and that could freestyle rap at any given moment on any given subject. Then there was Rick, a quiet Cape Verdean 20-something, who was as laid back as a reclining lawn chair. Then there was Henry, a quick-witted Jewish boy in his 20s, who ran the entire house, it seemed. And finally, Mike, a 20-something Navy Seal, who honestly didn't fit in any way. It was a mismatch of roommates, whom I called The Barnes Avenue Boys Club, who all shared the joy of smoking copious amounts of weed all day and night. Their kitchen was a complete mess and each guy had their own room with makeshift beds on the floor. BUT they had a pretty bad ass Apple computer, monitor, keyboard set up, so that was good enough for me.

Immediately, the guys came around and introduced themselves and I had gotten the feeling of me being Goldilocks and the guys being the three, curious little bears... and a Navy Seal. Anyway, they quickly understood exactly what I was going for sound-wise and we made plans to brainstorm and lay down tracks within the coming weeks. When you're young and are full of hopes and dreams, motivation comes easy.... unless well, you're high as fuck on THC.

Nonetheless, we worked together on a few tracks before we got sidetracked with the fact that I was an exotic dancer at The Foxy Lady. All of a sudden, the guys' ears perked up. It later came to my attention that the guys were actually part of a local drug ring selling weed, coke and ecstasy to the surrounding college kids in town. Henry was the ringleader for all this in that area and reported to a nerdy, Jewish, 30-something boss who lived a few blocks down and who liked to make his own cannabis-infused butter (pretty revolutionary at the time). He would would in turn get the supplies from a guy in Connecticut, who in turn got supplies from a guy in NYC. See, drug distribution is no different that another distribution business, it's set up like a pyramid scheme. Everyone had their local boss to report to. So, aside the fact that I had everyday encounters with druggie dancers, the guys were more interested in recruiting me as the sole supplier at The Foxy Lady.

At the time, I had a home loan to pay off (Sugar Daddy Tim had not yet paid it off for me, yet), so I was down as long as I didn't get caught. Before they could recruit me to run drugs in and out of the club, I had questions... lots of them. I told them I needed to get to know them better before I could do all that stuff... things were in jeopardy that I had worked hard for over the years. So, I hung out with Henry mostly and he showed me the different strains of weed and how to weigh and package them. Meanwhile, I was also doing gigs like The Chiller Convention in Connecticut with Troma, with the Barnes Avenue entourage tagging along. It was great! I had my own drugged out bodyguards. And then, on other nights, I would accompany them on their DJ gigs across southern New England...mostly illegal raves in abandoned factories.

Anyway, not only were we sidetracked from making music, we were sidetracked from keeping a low profile. One night, me and the Barnes Avenue Boys Club had plans to accompany Henry on one of his DJ gigs in Boston at The Roxy... 8pm passed by and there was no sign or phone call from the guys. 10 pm passed, no sign.... Midnight passed, no sign and the show had already began. Although it was unusual that they didn't call me to meet up and drive up to Boston together, I didn't really sweat it. I thought maybe one of them got messed up bad on drugs and canceled and they forgot to call me to let me know. No big deal.

The next morning, my mom was reading the Providence Journal and on the front cover I see" Drug Ring Bust in Providence" and there were photos of the cannabis butter guy and a few guys that I had met briefly and recognized! Holy Fuck!! The Barnes Avenue Boys Club got busted!! I was prudent to not to leave anymore messages on their phones or anything and kept my distance and laid low.

About a week after the bust, Navy Seal guy comes into The Foxy Lady looking for me. It was the end of my shift and we decided to meet at a restaurant so he can fill me in on what had happened. Did I mention it was Valentine's Day and had no plans? Anyway, the whole thing was fucking weird. Apparently, cannabis butter dude and the Barnes Avenue Boys were being monitored by the Feds for a while and moved in on a shipment exchange. Praise the fucking lord I wasn't with them! But what baffled me was, why wasn't Navy Seal dude not busted with them? It dawned on me that Navy Seal was probably a rat. A rat, giving information to the Fed's in return for whatever they promised him.... Immunity?? A salary?? More weed?? It was right there when I felt the need to leave to save myself.

Picking up on this feeling, Navy Seal said he wanted to take me to his car and take me somewhere for dessert. FUCK! Was he on to me knowing too much? Was he trying to set me up?? Was he going to kill me on Valentine's Day after he promised to take out for a sundae?? So, I obeyed and got in his car, thinking it was the end of me. We drove for about 10 minutes, which was the longest 10 minutes of my life and end up at Newport Creamery, a family diner chain that I had ironically worked at throughout high school as a waitress. So, I already knew the menu by heart... to which I ordered the 'Holy Cow' sundae, which happens to be biggest sundae ever, 10 scoops of ice cream, 4 toppings, whipped cream and 2 bananas accompanied by an unenthusiastic waitress ringing a cowbell in your face upon arrival of the sundae! If I was going to go out, I was going to go out on a sugar high. The sundae arrived and Navy Seal guy started grilling me about how much I knew and if I had run drugs into the club for them. I had not yet, luckily, and knew nothing and just kept eating the big ass sundae in front of me.

About 30 minutes later, I tell Navy Seal guy that I have to get going, to which he immediately replied, I'll drive you back to your car... omg, another long 10-minute drive back to my car, IF I'M LUCKY! We get to my car and I immediately jump out and politely thank him... and leave grateful and freaked out. I had made it another day.

About a month later, I read that Henry had gotten jail time and the other Barnes Avenue Boys had gotten a lighter sentence and probation. I'm not religious, but some kind of guardian angel was protecting me during those months... or maybe he just didn't want me making bad music... hahaha.

Chapter 30

SUSPICIONS GROW

I went right back to work at Mario's after the London trip with Tim during the Fall of 1999. My mother and brother were growing suspicious of my work. New cars, lavish gifts, European vacations from just waitressing in a bar wasn't adding up anymore. So, one night they cornered me and told me that they knew what kind of bar I was working at. I was mortified. I was like, 'I could NEVER be a dancer! You need freak show boobs to do THAT!'. Welp, they believed me once again. I did tell them about Tim and how I had a 'fan' that keeps buying me stuff. They looked more proud than mad. So, a few more months go by and finally, my mom had seen a huge suitcase full of my costumes in my trunk. It was a case of the mysterious suitcase in my trunk that really piqued their interest. Then I explained, sometimes I'm the 'shot girl' and I have to wear themed costumes. Yup! They bought that lie, too! I should've gotten a job in politics!

Shortly after that, my mother and brother said that they were going to stop by the club and visit that night. I was freaking out... so I told my boss I needed to waitress tonight. I ended up waitressing all night in what was a tuxedo playboy bunny outfit minus the ears. I explained to my clients my predicament and promised to see them next time. It was closing time and there was no sign of my family. Apparently, they did come, and the bouncer at the door wouldn't let them in because they were asking to see 'Roxanna', to which the bouncer said there's no Roxanna.... Makes sense, because everyone knew me by my STAGE name 'Tatiana'.

After my shift, I arrived home late at 2am and saw my mom and brother are up waiting for me. Shit. They called me a liar and cornered me into coming clean about where I really work. Well, I had enough of lying and I was over 18 so fuck them and let me live my life, right?! Well, I told them I was a stripper, yadda yadda, etc. They flipped out. So much so that my brother was throwing heavy bookends at me calling me a worthless whore and anything else degrading you can think of. That's when I called the police. They showed up, I didn't press charges and packed up my valuables because I didn't know if I'd ever come back to that house again.

I ended up staying the night with a fellow dancer friend of mine, Sabrina, a few towns over. I didn't sleep all night and thought I was going to have to marry Tim to make it though life. I honestly, had no idea how to live on my own even though financially, I was able to. To show you how dependent I was, I had built an addition on my mom's house just so I can stay. My family had three cats that we shared and one of the reasons why I had never moved out was because I couldn't bear to leave them, even though I had bought them and took care of them. My mother threatened to keep them if I moved out, which broke my heart. So, I stayed. I didn't realize I could go off and buy own house and live life alone. I even wanted to live in Vegas at one point and move in with my then boyfriend who was attending UNLV, but was just afraid of going out into the world like that ... alone. I always had wanted to be financially independent, but felt I still needed the safety net of my family and, of course the company of my beloved cats. I just didn't have the guts to go off on my own. I couldn't sleep and was sobbing all night.

Anyway, the whole situation sucked. The next morning after the incident, I got a call from my mother. She asked me to come back and hash things out. I figured I have to go back anyway to pack the rest of my stuff and figure out how we are going to figure out the finances of the addition I had just finished building. Her house was now a bonafide chateau because of my addition that included an entire wing of the house to myself with a marble-floored great room and bathroom with jacuzzi and custom walk-in closet. We sat down and spoke calmly. I told her everything…. how I would design my own costumes and shows, how much I was making, all the different clients I had… all of it. She looked at me with great admiration and proposed that I still live at the house seeing that I just dropped $50,000 cash to build an addition on her house, pay rent to her and in return, she would help me invest my money.

At the time, I was just making cash deposits weekly into three different locations of cash deposit boxes …. and I was running out of space. I really couldn't bank it anymore because the accounts had to have less than $10,000 in it in order not to tip off the IRS. So, I took the deal.

Within months, I had bought two foreclosed properties in Providence with the legal help of my mom. The properties would be in both of our names in return for her legal help. At the time, I was just thrilled that I could put my money into something solid with not much effort. For one of the properties, my mother and I had decided to turn it into a Bed & Breakfast. So, we spent one summer transforming a Victorian three decker house into a quaint, cute Bed & breakfast. It was a lot of work, but very fulfilling! We were repairing, painting and refurbishing old, vintage furniture for our new joint venture all financed by me.

By the spring of 1999, we had opened a six room Bed & Breakfast called The Providence Port Inn. It was a labor of love for sure and made me very proud. I was no longer just a stripper; I was a business owner. I was still dancing, of course. I still had to replenish the money we had spent renovating and what not. I also was my family's 'bank', if you will. They would come to me for a loan and would happily write them a check, no questions asked. If they paid me back, great, if not, it's ok… they were family. My mom got a BMW Z3; my brother had a few medical school bills… I also helped my mom get out of foreclosure on her house.

It felt good to have my work go toward things that were important, but I was getting older and grew tired of the stripper lifestyle. It's a hard lifestyle to keep up, especially as you get older. The thing about an industry that places importance on how you look is that it really fucks with your head. I was turning 24 soon and that was getting too old for the stripping business. There was always someone younger and pretty around the corner and I had to set myself up for a grand retirement and start a domestic life. It was time to find a husband. At least, that's what my mom would wisely say.

CHAPTER 31
END OF AN ERA

There comes a time in someone's life where you either stick with the status quo that no longer serves you or you take a risk and make a change. I was at a breaking point between quitting dancing, living in a stagnant place, and getting older. All my friends were moving on to other things, like getting married and moving on to other states for work. I was one of the first people in our group of friends to get married, but I still felt the pressure of getting on with my 'real' life of having a family and settling down. I was ready. How did I know I was ready? I was treating my cats like ACTUAL children! Well, I guess I think it was a clue I was ready.

Anyway, it's funny how when you're not looking, you find what you've been looking for. I was at the Sundance festival in 2002 when I met my current husband, Emmanuel. I was looking for a film director that could direct a film starring me financed by Tim. This actually would be the last hatched plan with Tim. I had retired from dancing two months prior and I was feeling like I needed one last set up. Already, I had an Amex expense card, my mortgage paid off and a paid off car- all courtesy of Tim, so I now wanted to fulfill my dreams of being in a real Hollywood film. I had the backing and now I just needed the director with the Hollywood connections.

After meeting my future husband at a Variety Party at Sundance (which I used Lloyd Kaufman's name to get in), we kept in touch while he sent me various scripts and projects. It was time to have Tim and Emmanuel meet face to face. I convinced Tim to take a business trip with me to Los Angeles to meet Emmanuel to discuss financing a film. I had my mother come along as a buffer. Tim had booked the rooftop suite of The Lux Hotel on Rodeo Drive. My mom and I had our own room and Tim had his own room connected with a common living /dining space. I could feel things were getting awkward and tiresome for Tim. Obviously, he wanted more from me, but I just wasn't interested in that way.

After a week of meetings, sight seeing and attending Hollywood premieres (courtesy of Emmanuel), we decided Emmanuel was the guy to help us. He sent us a variety of scripts to choose from that included horror, thriller and action. Emmanuel and I were strictly platonic, at this point. We kept in touch after his trip and agreed to meet in NYC a few weeks later. I could see things were falling apart with Tim, especially after he canceled my Amex card after a weekend in NYC without him. I was actually with Emmanuel that weekend in NYC.... and my situation with Emmanuel quickly turned non-platonic.

My sugar baby/sugar daddy relationship with Tim had gone a little sour after revealing that Emmanuel was pursuing me. I don't really blame Tim for feeling hurt. That wasn't my intention. But, I needed to move on and find my 'normal' life. I wouldn't say it ended on a bad note, but it wasn't a very happy one either. We remained cordial and I am eternally grateful for Tim- a man who was, literally, my Guardian Angel during a delicate time in my life.

The last time I saw Tim, I had met him in a parking lot where he gave me an envelope of cash and I told him I was marrying Emmanuel. I could tell he was heart broken, but not surprised. We gave each other a hug and went our separate ways.

I ended up being in a film with Emmanuel directing called "Scarecrow' a few months later that was financed by someone else. Three months later on October 27th, 2002, Emmanuel and I tied the knot in Providence, RI. I sold my Bed & Breakfast business and moved to California to start my new 'domestic' life with Emmanuel and went on to have three beautiful boys. I had started a new career as an international journalist (thanks to Emmanuel) and went on to film a few more features, while balancing the home life. A dream come true in many ways.

About a decade later, I had heard from Tim through Facebook. He had moved to somewhere in South America and had married a young lady in the region. I hope he has found happiness and a new lease on life.

After all that I have been through, I do feel gratitude for where I am today. Honestly, I'm surprised I never ended up dead in a ditch somewhere or worse, on the streets and in and out of jail. It always seems to me that I walk on the lucky side of life, despite all the dangers and risks I encounter.

Anyway, I thank you for making it this far in my book. As a wise person once said, "It feels good to be lost in the right direction." So, go on and live your best life doing it YOUR way. And remember to fuck them all! Not literally, only unless you want to…
XOXO,
Roxy

PHOTOGRAPHS 1995-2003

About the Author

Roxanna Bina is a writer, journalist, fashion blogger, and actress. She has interviewed celebrities on her Youtube Channel and written her fashion blog "Teacups and Couture" for the past 20 years. Her hobbies include ballet, fencing, and photography. She lives in sunny California with her husband whom she shares three sons with. Her other books include *"CATURDAY: Catnip For The Masses"*, *"Nightmares from the Dollhouse"* and *"Macabre Fairy Tales".*

www.RoxannaBina.com

www.ingramcontent.com/pod-product-compliance
Lightning Source LLC
Chambersburg PA
CBHW071356290426
44108CB00014B/1571